CONFERENCE ON BRITISH STUDIES
BIOGRAPHICAL SERIES

Editor: PETER STANSKY
Consultant Editor: G. R. ELTON

JOHN CARTWRIGHT

JOHN CARTWRIGHT

JOHN W. OSBORNE

RUTGERS UNIVERSITY

CAMBRIDGE

AT THE UNIVERSITY PRESS

1972

CAMBRIDGE UNIVERSITY PRESS
Cambridge, New York, Melbourne, Madrid, Cape Town, Singapore, São Paulo, Delhi

Cambridge University Press
The Edinburgh Building, Cambridge CB2 8RU, UK

Published in the United States of America by Cambridge University Press, New York

www.cambridge.org
Information on this title: www.cambridge.org/9780521085373

First published 1972
This digitally printed version 2008

A catalogue record for this publication is available from the British Library

Library of Congress Catalogue Card Number: 74–190422

ISBN 978-0-521-08537-3 hardback
ISBN 978-0-521-08814-5 paperback

TO MY WIFE

CONTENTS

PREFACE

This is the first book to be written about Cartwright since his niece, Frances Cartwright, published her *Life and Correspondence of Major John Cartwright* in 1826, two years after he died. I have tried to look at Major Cartwright primarily through his writings. He was not a politician like Joseph Hume, or a personality like Henry Hunt, or a behind-the-scenes operator like Francis Place. Insofar as he had any influence it was largely through the written word and even his letters are generally a reiteration of published opinions.

For reasons which I hope are made clear, Cartwright was not a success in his lifetime. This was due in part to his severe limitations as a thinker but also to the conditions of the time in which he worked. Still, the career of a person who did not achieve his objectives often provides us with valuable lessons. In the case of Cartwright we also have an example of a typical Englishman, a member of the landed gentry, striving to understand a world which was marked by deep and rapid change.

I wish to thank the authorities of the Houghton Library at Harvard University for allowing me to examine the fourteen volumes of Cartwright's own collection of his writings. The New York Public Library and the British Museum were equally generous in providing access to Cartwright materials. I am grateful to the Rutgers University Research Council for its support of my research. Thanks are also due to my wife for her patience and typing assistance.

JOHN W. OSBORNE

CHAPTER I

OLD ENGLAND AND THE FREE-BORN ENGLISHMAN

The England into which John Cartwright was born on 28 September 1740 resembled only superficially that country which he was to quit by death eighty-four years later. It is true that land was the main source of wealth and prestige during his long lifetime and that political dominance was exercised by an oligarchy during the reign of George IV as well as at the time of George II. The country would remain largely rural until well into the nineteenth century and such traditional institutions as the Church of England, Oxford and Cambridge universities and the legal system would suffer little or no change until after his death. But beneath the surface England had by 1824 undergone a great change and the youngster who had learned in youth of the 'forty-five', the War of the Austrian Succession and the introduction of the Gregorian calendar into England lived to witness the steam engine, the industrial city and demands for political democracy. Yet it is important to recognize that despite a family connection with applied steam power, John Cartwright never grasped the nature of the intimate relationship between the early Industrial Revolution, which took place during his lifetime, and politics. Even as a radical reformer Cartwright retained roots in that childhood England of Bonnie Prince Charlie and the Palladian Style, of smallpox and Squire Western.

Cartwright was born in Marnham in the county of Nottinghamshire, a region which was soon to be transformed by economic forces which were still gathering in the 1740s. The Cartwright family was solidly based in the county, having profited through a marriage connection with Thomas Cranmer, Henry VIII's ill-fated adviser. The family was still fairly prosperous although, like the Churchills, it had suffered for adopting the Royalist cause during the Civil War. Like other gentry families the Cartwrights had been victimized by the land tax. If the seventeenth century witnessed the rise of the gentry, the eighteenth century saw its decline. John was the third son in a family of five boys and five girls. His younger brother, Edmund, was to become the celebrated inventor of the power loom, a device which was to alter English life more than either man ever realized. John was sent first to a grammar school in Newark and then to Heath Academy in Yorkshire but he did not prosper as a student. Heath Academy may have been one of those cheap Yorkshire schools of the type which Dickens was later to castigate in *Nicholas Nickleby*. At any rate, Cartwright seldom referred afterwards to this experience and may have actually been lucky to emerge from it unscathed. Like so many of those to whom he later appealed, Cartwright was largely self-educated and throughout his life displayed the autodidact's characteristic confidence in his painfully acquired knowledge as well as a tendency to oversimplify difficult problems.

Spurning his parents' desire for him to help in the operation of the family farm, the young man wanted to leave home with the intention of entering the service of Frederick the Great, who was then approaching the height of his reputation as king of Prussia and military marvel of the age. Dissuaded from taking such a rash step, John nevertheless won permission to join the navy. Shortly after becoming part of the crew of the *Essex* he saw action when the ship captured a French frigate. Later he was posted as a midshipman to the *Magnamine*, which was under the command of Lord Howe and, while still a teenager, participated in the victory over the French of Quiberon Bay. In the thick of the action Cartwright saw half the men under his command killed or wounded and he himself suffered a slight wound. Sometime later he was to prove his courage once more by diving from the deck of a ship to rescue an officer who was in danger of drowning. At twenty-two he was appointed a lieutenant and the following year he received the command of a small ship. As a first lieutenant Cartwright was posted to Newfoundland in 1766.

During his career as a naval officer Cartwright pursued his duties with zeal and won the respect of his superior officers and the willing comradeship of his peers. While on active service in

Canada he engaged in extensive exploring expeditions but permanently injured his health as a result of physical over-exertion in the rugged climate. Although Cartwright was to outlive most of his contemporaries of these early years and amaze family and friends with his efforts during the last years of his life, it was a triumph of an iron determination over a weak constitution. The robust frame which he had taken to Canada was reduced to leanness and ever afterwards his face wore a pallid complexion. As a result of his North American experiences he also suffered from frequent illnesses. But in intervals between bouts of strenuous activity Canadian service did provide leisure for him to remedy some of the defects of his formal education by reading, and this practice he carried on after returning to England in 1770.

For the next four years impaired health confined Cartwright to shore-based activity. During these years he put his Canadian experiences to use by devising a scheme to secure a permanent supply of oak for the navy and discussing the rights of fishing companies. He also paid court to his future wife, Anne Dashwood, the daughter of a Lincolnshire gentleman. Despite his infirmities he had not given up hope of promotion in the navy and showed an awareness of the means through which such advancement was obtained by remaining on the best of terms with Lord Howe. Although there was little outward sign of the direction which his future life would take, his letters to his fiancée and to others indicated an appealing love of knowledge but also a self-confidence which at times approached smugness: 'Philosophical reading, and a habit of thinking rather closely, disqualifies one from enjoying ordinary or only tolerable poetry.'[1] This would be an unexceptional remark coming from an immature college student who had suddenly discovered the life of the mind, but Cartwright was a seasoned war veteran over thirty years of age. This enforced leisure was used wisely in self-improvement but the great morsels of knowledge which he gulped down were only imperfectly digested. The assured philosopher who was later to instruct or bore thousands was beginning to appear in

[1] F. D. Cartwright (ed.), *The Life and Correspondence of Major John Cartwright*, vol. I (London, 1826), p. 55. Hereafter cited as *L and C*.

the character of the beached naval officer. But in addition to reading Locke, Doddridge and Hume, Cartwright was also discovering the condition of politics in the country for which he had fought and this was the most important revelation of all.

Party politics in the eighteenth century was, as Alexander Pope sagely observed, 'the madness of many for the gain of a few'. A consequence of the Glorious Revolution of 1688 was the establishment of the ultimate supremacy of parliament over the monarch. Although the latter still retained extensive power and was far from being a figurehead, the mediocrity of Queen Anne and the first two Hanoverian kings, George I and George II, had permitted the legislature to gain power. While government was carried on in the king's name, he increasingly lost control of day-to-day political affairs to factions in parliament, which determined more and more questions of finance and patronage. Soon after Cartwright's birth, the prime minister, Sir Robert Walpole, would resign after a twenty-two year term of office and thus prove that the confidence of the House of Commons was as important to a chief minister as the good wishes of the monarch. An acute contemporary observer would look to the chambers of parliament rather than to the throne room of the royal palace for the seat of political action.

During this same period the Cabinet system had matured in order to overcome the constitutional problem which arose when parliament, although superior to the king, had no way of checking the daily work of the government except through the clumsy devices of impeachment and withholding money. The cabinet developed gradually in response to circumstances and was not the creation of abstract political philosophy. Described a hundred years later by Walter Bagehot as a 'buckle' between the executive and legislative branches of government, it made the monarchy more responsive to parliament. In a rough and ready fashion the cabinet had evolved from a group of personal advisers whom the Crown could consult as individuals either publicly or in private until in the reign of Queen Anne the link between cabinet and House of Commons began to form. For efficient government it became clear that the cabinet must be of the same party as the majority of the lower house; the Crown could not consult its advisers solely to suit its fancy. In an ill-defined way, although the cabinet was not responsible to the House of Commons, it was dependent upon that body. At the same time the first steps toward cabinet unanimity had begun to be taken. Anne's tendency to be governed by impulse rather than by reason made it difficult to do business with her, so members of her cabinet started to discuss matters among themselves before meeting the Queen and then present her with a united policy. By mid-century a new concept of the cabinet had emerged with the prime minister as the head of a body whose members controlled the administration and directed the legislative work of parliament as well. Only cabinet unanimity on all important issues remained to be achieved.

During this period of transition the fierce party strife of the later Stuarts had practically died away. The terms Whig and Tory had become little more than labels, with political life being carried on by shifting alliances based on family groups or self-interest. Also, after 1715 the cost of contesting elections rose, as there was increasing competition to get into parliament as a means of securing power and wealth. The exorbitant prices which were charged by voters for their support reduced the number of men in parliament with moderate incomes. At the same time the king's government had to resort to bribery by means of offices and sinecures in order to influence members of parliament, who had an acute sense of the advantages to be reaped by their position. This the Hanoverian monarchs could do, for although their powers were limited and not absolute, they still had authority to conduct foreign affairs and to make and unmake governments. Until 1760 there was no distinction between the king's private funds and public money. In the medieval fashion the monarch might thus dispose of vast sums without questions being asked. Also, in the absence of tightly knit parties and strict standards of political morality, the king could use his position as the fount of honour and the source of high office to his advantage.[1]

[1] For a discussion of politics at this time, see J. H. Plumb, *The Growth of Political Stability in England, 1675–1725* (London, 1967) and the two great works of Sir Lewis Namier, *The Structure of Politics at the Accession of George III* (2nd ed., London, 1961) and *England in The Age of the American Revolution* (2nd ed., London, 1961).

At this time the House of Commons consisted of 558 members, of whom 515 were from England and Wales. There was gross disproportion in the distribution of seats. Eligible voters in five south-western counties elected one quarter of the House of Commons and one of these counties, sparsely populated Cornwall, had only one less seat than all of Scotland. Apart from a handful of university seats, there were only two types of constituencies, counties and boroughs. Each county sent two representatives chosen under a uniform franchise that dated from the late Middle Ages. There was, however, no seeming rhyme or reason to support the various forms of borough franchise. These ranged from a few cases of universal male suffrage to seats where one person chose the two representatives all by himself. The borough representation had grown over the years. Many boroughs had received royal instructions to send representatives to Westminster centuries earlier when they had some economic or political importance. This they continued to do although many were in an extreme form of decay. In famous Old Sarum the two members were elected by the owner of a hill which had no buildings on it, while another borough, Dunwich, was partly under the sea and a third, Bishop's Castle, was the exclusive property of the East India Company. These 'rotten boroughs' were regarded as private possessions of their owners, but even where the right to vote was not a monopoly, bribery and vote-selling were customary and the boroughs with a fairly wide franchise were among the most corrupt. Less than 250,000 persons in Great Britain possessed the right to vote.

Some of the boroughs had once been thriving towns which had received their summons to send two members to parliament because of a flourishing commerce. Now insignificant, their political status remained unchanged while Manchester and Birmingham still had no representation. With every succeeding decade this anomaly became more evident. It was typical of a political ethos in which there was no real party system and little or no confrontation between political programmes or ideas. In the election of 1761, no contest was decided on the basis of party. The selfish interest groups, which included generals, admirals, lawyers and government contractors, as well as the more typical landed aristocracy or wealthy member of the gentry, believed that the least government was usually the best and were suspicious of changes that were not directly related to their concerns. Private business dominated the parliamentary calendar and oratory flourished in the absence of pressing national issues. Parochial rural values dominated politics as well as almost everything else in this society until the Industrial Revolution threw into ever bolder relief the obsolete pattern of the representation in the House of Commons. Meanwhile, the assertion that centres of increasing population and economic importance were either under-represented or had no direct voice at all in parliament were generally considered nearly as unwelcome as the advocacy of universal male suffrage.

Nepotism, sinecures and bribery were part of the game of politics. It was an expensive pastime in which only a few thousand out of the seven-and-one-half million people in Great Britain were fortunate enough to participate. But there was little clamour for reform. Practices which would impress the citizen of a civilized Western country in the twentieth century as being flagrantly corrupt were taken for granted by men of sensitivity and high character two hundred years ago. The ferment of advanced political ideas which developed during the Civil War had moderated considerably without entirely disappearing, and the word 'Radical' was not commonly used as a noun until after 1800. In fact, despite great inequalities and the presence of more poverty than later generations would tolerate, eighteenth-century England was a complacent country. It was victorious in war, had great overseas possessions and a thriving commerce. Above all, everyone took pride in the advantages of the English constitution in which there existed the rule of law with no room for absolute monarchy or *raison d'état*. The bureaucracy was weak, the rights of accused criminals were protected, there was no torture, and there was always an Opposition to the government of the day. This complacency was among the most powerful forces which had to be combatted by would-be reformers for the next two or three generations.

In addition to this deep and almost instinctual conservatism, the other major characteristic of mid-eighteenth-century English life was the profound respect which was paid to the rights of property. A legal code which increased the number of capital offences at a rate of more than one a year testified to a system of values under which the ruling classes staunchly guarded their possessions. People were executed for the theft of trifling sums in order to provide a warning to the rest of society.[1] Although the harshness of the law seemed to mock the claim of the Englishman that he lived in the freest country in the world, it was all of a piece: a man's vote was his property which could be sold or given to whomever he chose. It was necessary to have property to sit in the House of Commons, for only in this way could a person be considered to possess a stake in society. This was not an ancient reactionary dogma but a result of the Glorious Revolution of 1688. Ideas which favoured an extension of the right to vote to larger numbers of men had a harsh and uncongenial climate in which to work; proposals for reform of the political structure met a resistance which was based on more than self-interest.

It was the political state of affairs which Cartwright challenged in 1774 with his first purely political writing, *American Independence. The Glory and Interest of Great Britain.* This publication was dedicated to Sir George Saville (1726–84), a supporter of religious toleration, conciliation of the American colonies and a purer political life. Cartwright, who was still ambitious for promotion, was apprehensive that he might have jeopardized his chances but went ahead and had his pamphlet published. The work was certainly advanced for its time and may be regarded as the genesis of those political writings which he was later to wield as clubs against a usually indifferent government. Cartwright suggested a union between Great Britain and America similar to earlier proposals by the liberal-minded Real Whigs concerning England, Scotland, Wales and Ireland.[2] In this scheme both

[1] The criminal legal code is brilliantly depicted in Leon Radzinowicz's outstanding but frequently neglected *A History of English Criminal Law and its Administration from 1750*, vol. I, *The Movement for Reform, 1750–1833* (New York, 1948).

[2] Caroline Robbins, *The Eighteenth-Century Commonwealthman* (Cambridge, Mass., 1959), p. 10. Association with Real Whigs was to draw Cartwright into active politics.

America and the home country would have separate legislatures and the former could enjoy independence in taxation and trade. In the following year he stated his position succinctly in *A Letter to Edmund Burke, esq*. He advised the advocate of conciliation of the colonies that America should be admitted into partnership with England before she became a rival.[1] Rejecting the theory of virtual representation, Cartwright insisted that the Americans had the right to choose their own rulers and to tax themselves.[2] An enlightened view of colonies was always characteristic of this man. In a verbose, abstract style Cartwright repeatedly referred to 'natural justice' and 'established maxims of civil government' – themes which were to echo frequently in his subsequent writings. America could learn from the British constitution, but only by example and not by precept, as colonies were not children to be chastised by their mother. Cartwright predicted that eventually America would become fifteen independent kingdoms, but he was more accurate when he also prophesied that trade would not suffer as a result of the major political change which he upheld.

Despite Cartwright's assertions that the English parliament did not have sovereignty over America, the most striking fact which emerged from *American Independence* was the real concern expressed in it for the political condition of England. Cartwright was primarily interested in foreign policy as a tool with which to effect change at home. He was genuinely sympathetic to the Americans and totally devoid of any hint of opportunism, but he digressed so frequently into domestic politics that the effect of his effort was less a plan for America, than an urgent demand for reform in England. Although he disclaimed any admiration for that radical member of parliament, John Wilkes,[3] his correspondence at the time shows disillusionment not only with

[1] *A Letter to Edmund Burke, esq.* (London, 1775), p. 15. Cartwright thus went beyond Burke's famous conciliation speech.

[2] *American Independence* (London, 1774), pp. 6, 8–9, 17.

[3] *L and C*, vol. 1, p. 54. Wilkes had been arrested for publishing a libel on King George III. After years of agitation and litigation he was allowed to resume his seat in the House of Commons. It was an important victory for public opinion and individual liberty over corruption and bias. Cartwright was probably more upset by Wilkes' dissolute private life than his politics; he scarcely ever referred to him again.

government ministers but also with their supposed Opposition.[1] This accords with his reference to the House of Commons as 'the sink of corruption' and 'the putrid grave of the constitution'.[2] Corrupt elections, the inconsistency which meant that the boroughs of Dunwich and Old Sarum were as well represented as Norwich or Bristol and the cynicism of the late Sir Robert Walpole all come under criticism.[3] The Anglo-Saxon government, which was later to exercise such an immoderate fascination over his mind was not mentioned; in its place was an assertion that the source of liberty was God.[4] His letters contain references to too much ease and luxury bringing corruption, and this Jeremiah saw the state of politics as symbolic of the lost virtue of the English people. Cartwright's own Englishness was not demonstrated by the nature of his argument, which was neither at this time nor later as empirical and rooted in solid fact as he liked to believe. Instead it may be seen in his use of English models for illustrations of liberty. Cartwright's original lack of respect for foreign inspirations was changed by experience but at this time it was well indicated by his reference to the most renowned intellectual of the time, the mighty Voltaire, as 'the scribbling buffoon of Ferney'.[5]

His belief that God was the author of liberty rested upon a personal view of the deity. His niece and biographer claimed that Cartwright read the Bible daily and drew from it his own conclusions and he himself testified to apparent difficulties in religion being removed by resort to the scriptures.[6] References to God soon diminished in his political writings but Cartwright clung to a simple non-denominational faith to the end of his days. In the same manner his views on politics changed very little over the decades. Believing that politics had a firm basis in the laws of God and nature, Cartwright insisted that the line between right and wrong was as sharp in this sphere as it was in personal conduct. The principles of political behaviour were self-evident even for the simple person: there were no complexities which

[1] *Ibid.* pp. 55, 58.

[2] *American Independence*, pp. v–vi.

[3] *Ibid.* pp. v–vii, 42.

[4] *Ibid.* pp. 7, 39.

[5] *Ibid.* p. x.

[6] *L and C*, vol. I, p. 179; vol. II, p. 287.

would excuse wrongdoing. Since everything was potentially clear, it remained only for the political philosopher to remove the encumbrances which had been scattered over and around the truth and the people would proceed toward correct principles of political behaviour as though guided by a compass. Like Luther in religion, Cartwright had an over-simplified opinion of the self-evidence of truth. He was, however, firmly convinced that his mission in life was to clarify that which was always there rather than to innovate with bold new ideas.

Cartwright's political opinions did not prevent him from being appointed a major in the Nottinghamshire militia in 1775, the same year in which he published a second edition of *American Independence*. The appointment provided him with the title by which he was known afterwards, although he was deprived of his commission in 1792. Cartwright was characteristically zealous in the pursuit of his duties and was especially ready to instruct others in theirs. He drew up a small manual of instruction for the use of officers and non-commissioned officers, and the portion which pertained to the former was marked by a freedom from the inconsistencies and redundancies which frequently marred his political writings. By efficiency, dignity, and self-control the officer was to inspire pride and respect for authority in the common soldier. Cartwright's later career makes it clear that he was never an egalitarian or a social leveller: in this case, the officer must be set apart from his men, but he must be ever-mindful of his responsibility and set an example of obedience, punctuality and attention to details. The writer of these reflections demonstrated his own capacity for the latter by designing a regimental button which showed a cap of liberty resting on a book over which appeared a hand holding a drawn sword. The motto read 'Pro legibus et libertate'. In the context of the French Revolution such an act would have been considered almost treasonous but in the more genial climate of the 1770s it seems to have provoked no negative reaction.

These parochial concerns were soon to be overshadowed by the approach of war with the American colonies when Cartwright would reach a turning point in his life. Lord Howe, upon being appointed commander-in-chief of the navy and commissioner to America, wrote to Cartwright and offered him a lieutenancy on board his own ship. In a letter to his fiancée Cartwright revealed an awareness of the opportunity which he had within his grasp. 'I believe that the command of so many ships never fell to the lot of one man, since the defeat of the Spanish Armada; so it will be the fairest field for promotion that can be imagined.'[1] Yet despite his love of the navy, respect for Lord Howe and natural concern for his career, Cartwright declined the appointment. Convinced of the justice of the American cause, his integrity would not permit service under these conditions. In a letter to Lord Howe Cartwright expressed his scruples in respectful language and then forwarded to the commander-in-chief a copy of *American Independence*. He received in reply a short but friendly note in which there was no evidence that Howe had read Cartwright's tract. A subsequent exchange of correspondence only confirmed the friendly parting.

Having refused this splendid opportunity for promotion, Cartwright's patriotism led him to decline as well an offer to serve in the American navy. At thirty-six years of age he had reached a point when most men are settled in their life's work, but Cartwright's real career was only beginning. As an indefatigable political pamphleteer he was to instruct an English public which was usually uninterested and sometimes hostile in its heritage of political liberty and in the necessity of making this liberty the criterion for the widespread change which he deemed necessary. The American Revolution brought into the open his doubts about the wisdom of continuing current practices (though he retained faith in the validity of ancient constitutional ideas). Once this happened he was a marked man. In the face of government opposition toward his views Cartwright could not expect to enjoy the career as a navy officer which had once seemed so promising.

Thus, as early as 1776 he took a position against the *status quo* in politics. The message contained in *American Independence* was to be expanded and developed later, but perhaps not as much as one might expect. Of more interest are the character

[1] *Ibid.* vol. I, p. 73.

traits which were always to stamp the work of Major John Cartwright: a stalwart integrity which drew admiration from all generous-minded opponents and an indomitable perseverance in the face of a half century of adversity. Sure of his principles, Cartwright laboured consistently to impart his reasoning to others. But even here in these early years as a rather solemn political gadfly there are traces of the didacticism which led many people to dismiss him as a humourless pedant. This condition may have been caused by his inadequate education. Certainly the self-taught philosopher had a rather narrow foundation in historical learning upon which to erect such a substantial temple of political thought.

Cartwright's sterling personal qualities were linked with his career as a political writer. Rising at six, he worked until almost three in the afternoon. His exercise and recreation were as moderate as his frugality at the dinner table. Generous toward the failings of others, his own character was stalwart; right and wrong were clearly defined and the line between the two did not blur. Subtlety and equivocation never were his distinguishing marks and he showed the same life-long loyalty to the moral principles of his youth as he did toward the small clothes which went out of fashion for most men during the French Revolution.[1] Thoughtful, courteous and obliging, Cartwright was, with his unobtrusive religious faith and restrained manner of address, an example of the finest type of eighteenth-century English gentleman.

While Cartwright could never overcome either his educational deficiencies or the lack of a high intelligence which made the former more evident, he was not negligible as a thinker. Later issues were to reveal a mind which, if it was neither penetrating nor nimble, was tenacious and even had a touch of originality. His career disproved Cartwright's frequent assertions that he desired nothing new in politics. Above all, the man who inspired generosity in the judgment of others was unusually generous himself, and it is appropriate that, since the last great issue at the close of his life would be South American independence, his

[1] The *Annual Register*, vol. 66 (1824) published a short obituary which stressed Cartwright's steadfast qualities. See page 233.

career should open by championing the cause of Britain's North American colonies.

Despite having left home at an early age, Cartwright remained at heart a landed gentleman and would purchase land himself when he had an opportunity to do so. His writings were coloured by a partiality for agriculture as a way of life and, as he grew older, by a deepening prejudice against commercial interests. Many of his early associates in the cause of reform were nostalgic gentry who shared Cartwright's feelings. At a time when living standards were rising many of the gentry were discontented. Some were being driven to the wall, forced to sell out to larger landowners; others were simply not prospering in proportion to the magnates or newly rich bankers, brokers, lawyers and holders of government securities. Much of their distress was due to nearly twenty years of war against France during the reigns of William and Anne, which they paid for with their taxes while commercial interests thrived. No wonder business was looked upon suspiciously. The reaction was profound and long-lasting and included a conspiratorial theory of politics in which the government had succumbed to finance.

In the early part of the eighteenth century Henry St John, Viscount Bolingbroke, was the spokesman of those who opposed land taxes, the national debt, the Bank of England, moneyed interests, stockjobbers and English soldiers being sent on overseas campaigns.[1] These were all live political issues a hundred years later. Hatred of finance capital, a desire for economy in government expenditures, parliament being summoned more frequently, resentment over the standing army and suspicion of foreigners represented a rich vein in English life.[2] It produced a desire to return to a glorious past and a demand for radical reform to achieve this goal. Cartwright was very much a part of this movement. We shall meet this spirit many times in his writings.

One of the results of this state of mind was a dislike for the

[1] Isaac Kramnick, *Bolingbroke and His Circle* (Cambridge, Mass., 1968), pp. 9–10.

[2] For example, a tract written when Cartwright was a child: *A Winter Evening's Conversation in a Club of Jews, Dutchmen, French Refugees and English Stockjobbers at a Noted Coffee House in Change Alley* (London, 1748).

Glorious Revolution by many men who were not Jacobites. Acclaimed by the followers of that great Establishment figure, Sir Robert Walpole, to others the events of 1688 and 1689 represented the beginnings of corruption in government, high taxation and an increase in the influence of finance capital. Cloaked in nostalgia, Cartwright and his associates in several seemingly progressive political groups in the 1780s and 1790s wanted an end to this as well as the restoration of a citizen militia.[1] This was the view of an alienated out-group in society, some of whose members would return to orthodoxy for patriotic reasons after 1789 (and also because agricultural conditions improved), but others would remain embittered.

While the first spokesman for this group was the profligate aristocrat, Bolingbroke, the last was the son of a small farmer and innkeeper, William Cobbett. It was the latter's misfortune to write his inspired prose at the worst possible time and thus fail to arouse enough of the discontented gentry to be a real threat to successive Tory governments, which were allied with commerce, until several years after Waterloo. Things did change in the 1820s and 1830s but not in the direction that Cobbett wanted. Cartwright, who had a loose alliance with Cobbett, died in 1824, eight years before the passage of the Great Reform Bill. Regarded today as one whose agitation made this and other progressive legislation possible, Cartwright would have been unhappy had he lived to see more power in the hands of men whom he distrusted. Urban, middle-class England of the Victorian age was certainly not the ideal society which he had in mind when he was writing his books and pamphlets.

Yet when Cartwright's career is seen in the entire perspective of modern British history it is clear that this man was far from being a failure. Cartwright was more than an eighteenth-century gentleman whose ideas had been formed early in life and who did

[1] This theme is well discussed for the early part of the century in Kramnick, *Bolingbroke*, passim. Under different circumstances a similar mentality may be observed in the socialist Robert Blatchford (1851–1943), a man with affinities toward Maurras and *L'Action Française* and Lueger's Viennese Christian Socialists. See Bernard Semmel, *Imperialism and Social Reform, English Social–Imperial Thought, 1895–1914* (New York, 1968), p. 216. The politics of nostalgia is far from dead in contemporary England. See George Thayer, *The British Political Fringe* (London, 1965).

not learn much from experience. A statue of him in London testifies to the respect and affection in which he was held by his middle-class colleagues; but his real legacy is twofold. In the course of his career he advanced certain ideas, one or two of which were entirely original (for example, universal male suffrage). These were to become part of the constitution. Perhaps of even more importance was the atmosphere of sanity and moderation which, in general, marked his work and reflected Cartwright's personal decency. Although representing a minority viewpoint, he contributed to that remarkable absence of hatred and violence characteristic of the English reform movement. If an important measure of the quality of life in a country is its ability to accommodate to change without severe disruption, then Cartwright's work may be regarded as successful. In his writings there is much that is retrograde and irrelevant but the overall impression is of humanity and charity.

CHAPTER 2

THE EMERGING RADICAL

The American Revolution provided an inspiration for Englishmen who were dissatisfied with the state of their constitution. Although the arguments of the American patriots did not have any great ideological impact, their discontent acted as a leaven for change. Before the reign of George III the political complaint that was most frequently heard was a demand for more frequent parliaments than those provided by the Septennial Act of 1716.[1] This was an appropriately tame issue with which to launch an attack upon the state of politics. The activities of John Wilkes in the late 1760s were generally directed at being re-elected to parliament after having been expelled for attacking government policy in his paper, *The North Briton.* The issue of a free press and the rights of a constituency to choose its own representative were recognized as important by the electors of the county of Middlesex (one of the most sophisticated groups of voters in Great Britain) to whom Wilkes wisely appealed in his effort to get reinstated to the House of Commons. But after Wilkes was successful in taking his seat in 1774 he failed to demonstrate vigour in pressing for reform. Other issues also did not strike sparks and the political atmosphere was torpid until the American demands gradually made some persons in England think seriously about their country's future.

The year 1776, which saw the publication of *The Declaration of Independence*, Adam Smith's *The Wealth of Nations*, Jeremy Bentham's *Fragment on Government*, and the opening volumes of Gibbon's *Decline and Fall of the Roman Empire*, also witnessed the appearance of a short book by Cartwright entitled *Take Your Choice!*[2] It was to be Cartwright's most famous book and contained the basis of most of his political philosophy. During

[1] Carl B. Cone, *The English Jacobins* (New York, 1968), p. 40.

[2] In the 1780 edition, which is used here, the title read *The Legislative Rights of the Commonalty Vindicated; or, Take Your Choice!*

the next five decades the former naval officer was to preach essentially the same message and to make as few tacks as possible in the course which he had charted, whether the wind was fair or foul. Always self assured, he continually asserted the timelessness of his programme. Warning that those who act on wrong principles are doomed to unhappiness, he claimed, 'It is not so with those who act on right principles. Seeing themselves neglected or ridiculed, finding themselves foiled in all their attempts, and feeling the sacrifices they make to their duty, they are yet happy in themselves; they enjoy the tranquillity within, and they taste the supreme of all earthly delights, the love and esteem of the virtuous.'[1] Nor was *Take Your Choice!* unworthy to rank in daring, and even influence, with those works of the year 1776 whose genius has been authenticated by time. Although Cartwright was familiar with contemporary radical thought and quick to seize other men's points and extend them, he added original ingredients of his own. In the course of his discussion Cartwright helped to shape the policies which were to influence the mainstream of British radicalism until the middle of the nineteenth century: an avoidance of violence, emphasis upon political rather than economic issues, the importance of the past as a guide to the present and a subtle anti-egalitarianism. His specific ideas not only anticipated the Chartist platform of the late 1830s and 1840s, but some of them continue to resound today.

In *Take Your Choice!* he used the quarrel with America as an excuse to examine the health of the British constitution. Quickly calling war with the colonies unjust and thus disposing of that issue, Cartwright subjected the state of politics to scrutiny. He began with an analysis in which he saw the two political parties distinguished from each other only by cant terms. 'The bulk of partizans on each side, foolishly enlist themselves under the opposite leaders, from hereditary habits, from family attachments, from academical prejudices, from views of interest or ambition, and, indeed, from all sorts of motives, except those of solid convictions, upon serious and impartial examinations into the tenets of both parties.'[2] In spite of this, he still regarded the

[1] *L and C*, vol. 1, p. 102.

[2] *Take Your Choice!*, p. vii.

Whigs as more likely to reform than the Tories and appealed to them from time to time in the course of his narrative. As in all of his sustained writing, an insistence upon 'reasoning closely' is belied by the loose structure of the argument. Cartwright's ability as a political theoretician was minimal; he was both unhistorical and prone to draw false conclusions from weak premises. Perhaps his greatest significance as a thinker was his ability to foresee certain specific demands of future generations. In this respect *Take Your Choice!* is remarkable for it recommends manhood suffrage, voting by ballot, annual elections, equal electoral districts and even looks ahead to the abolition of property qualifications for members of the House of Commons as well as the payment of salaries to these members.[1] Cartwright's confident assertion that these constitutional changes derived from the working of '*common sense* upon self-evident propositions' was as inaccurate as his claim that annual parliaments and equal electoral districts were ancient practices.[2] Autodidacts tend either to despise theory and therefore ignore it altogether or to becloud their thoughts with dubious premises. Cartwright clearly fell into the latter group.

The beliefs that men were created equal by God and that liberty rather than dominion was held by divine right were characteristic of the shaky foundation of much radical political thought of the time, whether the location was England, France or America. Exposing the weaknesses of the *a priori* method of reasoning was easy for political conservatives, but even the great Edmund Burke could not offer an explanation (except that of general human fallibility) for the appeal of these arguments to many intelligent men, nor could they substitute more concrete formulations of their own (save those of experience). Demonstrated human weakness and validity by presumption are legitimate and powerful checks upon rash innovation and they were fully employed. But although Cartwright and his fellow radicals failed to make clear why annual parliaments would be more unselfish and public spirited than septennial ones, neither could it

[1] *Ibid.* passim. The last two points were not contained in the 1776 edition.

[2] *Ibid.* pp. 17–18.

have been proved that they would not have been an improvement. Cartwright was frequently illogical but he was not necessarily incorrect in asserting that major change could be introduced into government without disastrous consequences. Like Burke, he believed in an essentially organic society but did not construe this as an excuse to refrain from reform.

Cartwright was not absorbed in the theory which influenced many of George III's political enemies: that there was a conspiracy of king's friends to subvert the constitution. This myth was publicized by Edmund Burke in his *Thoughts on the Causes of the Present Discontents*, which was published in 1770. The pamphlet impressed some fearful men for it suggested that the puzzling actions of the government could be explained by the machinations of obscure but potent figures at court who were using the influence of the crown for the aggrandizement and enrichment of themselves to the detriment of the country.[1] Unlike most radical writers Cartwright at the time had little to say about the king and seems not to have been very much influenced by the Wilkes case. The mysteries of court intrigue did not interest him and a peculiarity of his writing at this time was that it paid little attention to topical issues of domestic politics. Specific techniques of agitation, however, he did borrow from others.

To Cartwright a large army and a high national debt were not necessary and the war against America was unjust. Annual parliaments, in his opinion, would not have permitted these evils.[2] Here, as in later writings, he does not seek scapegoats. A mark of Cartwright's thinking is its concentration upon forms of government and not upon personalities. Surely no radical was ever more generous to political opponents or so unwilling to argue *ad hominum*. Given the unfavourable circumstances in which the country found itself he believed that almost any change in the political structure was bound to be beneficial, yet there was no disposition to blame any persons in particular for these conditions. Beneath the cloudy abstractions which hovered over

[1] This idea is discussed in chapter 1 of *Myth and Reality in Late Eighteenth-Century British Politics and Other Papers* by Ian Christie (Berkeley and Los Angeles, 1970).

[2] *Take Your Choice!*, pp. xvii–xviii.

Take Your Choice! lay a firm faith in England's ancient constitution and a reluctance, which should not be confused with timidity, to engage in a discussion of the frailties of specific individuals.

Cartwright's specific political remedies also show evidence of a generous mind: annual parliaments whose members would have the interests of the nation at heart, distinction between human beings should be by mind and morals rather than birth, and poverty should not be a bar to voting. The right to vote should be permitted to eighteen-year-olds because of their being eligible to serve in the militia.[1] He could not bring himself to discard either monarchy or aristocracy but, on the other hand, the man who rejected virtual representation would not allow a woman the right to vote on the ground that her husband represented her.[2] Representation should be by the number of voters in a town, except for places with very small populations which should be included in the county voting list. Although the House of Lords would retain its hereditary nature, the total number of peers should be in proportion to the population of the country. Every 1 June voting would be held under the supervision of parish officers and the sheriff of each county. For a person who looked forward to the abolition of financial and property qualifications for voting, his requirements for candidates for the House of Commons were high. Each county member must have a landed estate plus £400 per annum. In London the requirement was the same or else property valued at £12,000. To represent other cities and towns a candidate must possess £300 a year in land or £9,000 in other property.[3]

These innovations were to be made only for the sake of improving the quality of political life in the country, and to this end Cartwright professed himself willing to substitute other forms if it could be demonstrated that they would be more efficacious. Noteworthy also are his allusions to the classics of English political thought – especially the writings of Locke – and the continued lack of interest in Continental political theorists. He certainly misread many of his sources but the

1 *Ibid.* pp. xvi, 5, 30, 147–8.
2 *Ibid.* p. 46.
3 *Ibid.* pp. 149–65.

choices which he made were characteristic of a man who always retained faith in the essential rightness of English political forms and scorned advice from abroad. As Anglo-Saxon institutions soon made their appearance in his writing in a garbled form the references to Locke disappeared. Not so, however, his antagonism to the Glorious Revolution, which continued to draw his ire for failing to guard the people's liberties.[1] However, the exclusively English inspiration was there from the beginning.

In addition to the continued resentment against the Glorious Revolution, Cartwright emerges in *Take Your Choice!* as a believer in a society in which classes are flexible and individual merit may be rewarded; hence the belief that mind and morals rather than birth must distinguish a human being. He even goes so far as to assert that no one deserves elevation unless it is given by his fellows.[2] He never did like the House of Lords and was cool toward the monarchy as well. Here, in 1776, he evades a direct confrontation but the tone of his later writing is set. By no means an egalitarian, Cartwright had the independence of the country gentleman toward established authority. The growth of his interest in Anglo-Saxon England may perhaps be seen as a corollary of this fact.

This is clearly indicated in *Take Your Choice!* which shows Cartwright's indebtedness to men such as Obadiah Hulme, whose *Essay on the English Constitution* (1771) considered Anglo-Saxon democracy to be the political ideal and who pleaded for annual elections, the secret ballot, and an extension of the suffrage. James Burgh in his three volume *Political Disquisitions* (1774–5) had made demands similar to Hulme's and, in addition, proposed a National Association to bring grass roots pressure for reform upon parliament. This extra-parliamentary scheme won wide acceptance among radicals of the time and influenced such important nineteenth-century movements as Chartism and the Anti-Corn Law League. Hulme and Burgh received scant mention from Cartwright in his writings. A more versatile thinker than Cartwright, John Jebb, was already active in proposing legal, penal and university reform as well as equal

[1] *Ibid.* p. xxxi.

[2] *Ibid.* p. 3.

electoral districts, universal male suffrage and annual parliaments.[1] The two men were to become friends. Cartwright's only original contribution may have been his advocacy of an unalloyed universal manhood suffrage. On this issue he was explicit and meant to be taken literally. Although he believed that in practice the lower orders would defer to their social superiors and, anyway, would be too jealous to permit one of their number to be raised to high station,[2] the right of every man to vote was inherent in his personality.

Cartwright was thus part of a very limited concern for reform which antedated the 1770s but crystallized around the cause of the American revolutionaries. During the next few years he wrote a couple of brief pamphlets on behalf of their struggle against English imperialism,[3] urging a reconciliation between America and England. The first real indication of the nascent reform movement was to come in 1780, the year when the most complete edition of *Take Your Choice!* was published. By this time war-weariness and disgust with the peccant political system had spread into quarters previously regarded as solidly behind the *status quo*. In April of that year Dunning's famous resolution that 'the influence of the Crown has increased, is increasing, and ought to be diminished' was carried in the House of Commons. Although it led to nothing in the way of major political change, Dunning's resolution was symptomatic of a state of mind which produced a brand of fiscal and administrative reform in the next few years that indirectly whittled down the powers of the monarch. Indeed, these powers were being diminished while Dunning spoke, and the Crown was less influential then than at the ascendancy of George III.

At the same time, an Anglican clergyman, the Reverend

[1] See Cone, *English Jacobins*, Robbins, *Commonwealthman*, and E. C. Black, *The Association, British Extraparliamentary Political Organization, 1769–1793* (Cambridge, Mass., 1963) and Ian Christie, *Wilkes, Wyvill and Reform, The Parliamentary Reform Movement in British Politics, 1760–1785* (London, 1962) for brief discussions of the activities of these men. Cartwright seldom referred to them in his publications.

[2] *L and C*, vol. 1, pp. 84–5.

[3] *The Memorial of Common-Sense upon the Present Crisis Between Great Britain and America* (1778), and *A Letter to the Earl of Abingdon*, etc. (1778). The pamphlets stress that America was lost to English rule, but might be retained as a friend and ally against the French.

Christopher Wyvill, was leading a group of sober Yorkshire gentry and clergy into a denunciation not only of extravagant government expenditure but primarily of the unscrupulous nature of politics and the great power of the executive. Wyvill's group, the Yorkshire Association, favoured an end to the incompetently managed war and desired triennial parliaments, economy in government, and a modest extension of the franchise to the propertied middle class. These ideas were not as important as the support of the Yorkshire Association by beef-eating, port wine-drinking squires and parsons and the success of the Association in gaining temporary control of this great county from the aristocracy. It was the first effective extension of political radicalism from London to the provinces. The Yorkshire Association technique of county meetings influenced Cartwright, although he was irked by Wyvill's unshakable moderation – a personality characteristic which resembled his own unshakable radicalism.[1]

There were groups at the time which had more radical aims than the modest ones of the Yorkshire Association. Indeed, while Dunning was presenting his resolution to parliament, a band of reformers which had been instructed by Charles James Fox to prepare a programme for reform was already at work. Fox was the leader of the Westminster Committee, and it was a subcommittee of this body which included Jebb and Cartwright, that produced a report going beyond the desires of its rather shifty sponsor. Fox had deliberately appointed men more radical than he to the subcommittee in the hope of capturing the leadership of this budding movement for reform from Wyvill. For his own part, Cartwright's appointment represented his emergence on the political scene as a framer of policy, as well as his first connection with 'radical Westminster', a borough whose 9,000 voters were perhaps the most intelligent as well as among the most numerous groups of electors in the kingdom. In later years Cartwright was to strive in vain to represent this constituency in the House of Commons.

[1] Christie, *Wilkes, Wyvill and Reform*, presents a more favourable view of Wyvill than one is apt to receive from a study of Cartwright's writings.

The report of the subcommittee called for universal male suffrage, annual parliaments, equal electoral districts, a secret ballot, single member constituencies, abolition of property qualifications for membership in the House of Commons and payment for members of the lower house. The congeniality of Cartwright's ideas to the rest of the subcommittee is obvious, as is the report's inspiration for future generations of reformers. Yet as Carl Cone has recently pointed out, the idea that members of the lower orders would ever be elected to the House of Commons was beyond eighteenth-century comprehension.[1] Except for Cartwright the members of the subcommittee construed universal male suffrage to mean ratepayer suffrage and they were not favouring the right of paupers or household servants to vote. It has been noted that even Cartwright did not grasp the implications of his proposals in terms of those who might actually be elected. The majority of the Westminster Committee, which included many prominent members of parliament, were by no means as radical as the subcommittee. Their absence or infrequent attendance at meetings spoke as loudly as words.

There is one other contribution to this edifice of radicalism to consider before the entire structure was damaged during the Gordon riots of June 1780. This was the founding on Cartwright's initiative of the Society for Constitutional Information in April 1780. Other members of this group besides Cartwright included Jebb, Granville Sharp, Capell Loftt, Hollis, the Duke of Richmond, Richard Brinsley Sheridan, the Whig playwright, and Dr Richard Price, a non-conformist minister, whose enthusiasm for the French Revolution a decade later was to provoke Burke's *Reflections on the Revolution in France*. The SCI was dedicated to political reform but was far from democratic in composition, as there was a minimum annual subscription of one guinea. It was one of those amorphous, well-meaning organizations which in a later century would be attacked by adherents of a more thoroughgoing, if less humane, radicalism. The membership was united behind the necessity of political reform but little else. The SCI was not egalitarian, did not

[1] Cone, *English Jacobins*, pp. 58–9.

believe that government had any duty to improve the physical well-being of its citizens and was not concerned with the economic needs of the humble. In other words, this was a characteristic idea of liberal-minded, eighteenth-century gentlemen: rhetorical and rooted in ancient political tradition. It was to be found wanting by the Painite radicalism of the 1790s and expire in 1794 during a period of black reaction when any proposal of change was suspected of being treason.[1]

The purpose of the SCI was to educate the English people in the heritage of their own political liberty. To this end the society printed and distributed without charge classics of political philosophy, as well as works relating to contemporary affairs written by its members. A very popular figure among these radicals was the reactionary Bolingbroke, whose nostalgia for a simpler society was appealing to them. Political reform was held to be necessary if the noble traditions of English freedom were to be preserved from usurpation. In general, the members wanted an extension of the franchise, more frequent elections, a restriction on the power of the monarch and House of Lords, and the elimination of bribery and corruption in the nation's political life. A demand for lower taxes was also advanced, a reminder to modern readers that here and for a long time afterward 'radicalism' stood for small, inexpensive government. The routine appeal for religious toleration was unwisely broadened by some members to an attack upon the established church. This immoderate assertion by a minority was used against the SCI by its enemies, who claimed that Throne and Altar, Church and State were in danger from this band of unscrupulous radicals. English to the core, it must be reiterated that the SCI was a product of the sunny political climate of the age of Johnson, with its freedom of expression and official tolerance of eccentricity. It was doomed in the darker atmosphere after 1789. Moderate as it was, the leaders of the SCI were spurned by Wyvill who tried to cooperate

[1] See G. S. Veitch, *The Genesis of Parliamentary Reform* (Hamden, Connecticut, 1965) passim, for a description of the SCI. Veitch's book was originally published in 1913 and some of his judgments are out of date. See the introduction by Ian Christie in the above edition. Also, see Cone, *English Jacobins*, pp. 212–13 on the dissolution of the SCI.

instead with the Rockingham faction. As a measure of the SCI's moderation the Society urged its members during the Gordon Riots to organize themselves for the defence of property.

The Gordon Riots, which broke out after Lord George Gordon and his small band of followers urged the people to protest against a few trivial concessions to Roman Catholics, resulted in hundreds of deaths and immense property damage in London alone. When the extensive anti-Catholic prejudice of the people had been expressed, the mob turned against the homes and businesses of wealthy merchants, the Bank of England was threatened, the gates of prisons opened and during an orgy of alcohol and fire London was subjected to sack. Only after a week was order restored and those who participated in or witnessed the events never forgot what had happened. One aspect of the riots was the seeming concentration of the rioters on the persons and property of the well-to-do, another was the weakness of the police forces. From a long range point of view the Gordon Riots brought home to an all-too-complacent generation the festering misery and resentment in the capital and the inadequacy of the forces of law and order. The events of this week in June led neither to social reform nor to the strengthening of the police. These objectives were only accomplished at a later time and for different reasons. But the fear which had been engendered never entirely disappeared. It would be a mistake to see the swing to intense conservatism as beginning in 1790 or 1791; the timid reforms of the 1780s and the lukewarm reception accorded to advanced political ideas was in part due to a subtle fear of what could occur when the rigid bonds which held society together were relaxed. This reaction temporarily diminished the pressure of the reformers on the government and created problems of respectability for the groups which had urged change. Cartwright and his associates never grasped the fact that the altered state of mind made imperative a new basis for political reform.

The first edition of *Take Your Choice!* led to correspondence with Richard Price and also with the Duke of Portland, who flirted with liberal ideas before settling down during the French Revolution as a disciple of Edmund Burke. Price had also published in 1776. *Observations on The Nature of Civil Liberty, The Principles of Government and The Justice and Policy of the War with America* was perhaps his chief, if not best known, political work and in it he held a position on the American question similar to Cartwright's. The latter, with a substantial contribution to the political debate to his credit, tried to interest various members of the nobility, including Lord Shelburne, to take the lead in the movement for reform. In this he was unsuccessful. Ever sanguine, Cartwright judged the amount of zeal possessed by others in terms of his own ample bounty and experienced persistent disappointments which might have crushed the spirit of another man. A few years later he was to be chagrined by the failure of Dunning's motion to ignite more reform than Burke's economical measures; here, in the late 1770s, he sought in vain for a man who could rally the discontented around a standard.

An opportunity soon appeared to present itself for the new pamphleteer to serve in parliament. At the end of 1778, some burgesses of the town of Nottingham invited him to run for a seat in the House of Commons, but at the last moment the nomination was given to one of their number. Cartwright, who had received the freedom of the town two years previously, was disappointed and his feelings were further lacerated when a chance to be a candidate for Nottingham county was lost, with the Duke of Portland supporting his opponent. Although his niece implies that it was her uncle's purity of character and devotion to the public good which cost him this chance,[1] the electors may have been influenced by other than sordid motives. Cartwright would not have been either a particularly good candidate or, if elected, an able representative. His formal speeches bored listeners. Like Dorothea Brooke's uncle in *Middlemarch* he could not think quickly on his feet, and he consistently lacked practical political sense. Slow and ruminative, Cartwright excelled only in writing long pamphlets in which he could marshall his ideas slowly and deploy them at his own speed. Two years later he stood for election at Nottingham but lost badly.

[1] *L and C*, vol. 1, p. 124.

Cartwright's activity was not limited to the political sphere. During these years he also served in the militia and drew up plans to defend Portsmouth against enemy attack. In 1779 he showed versatility by devising a scheme to calculate the positions of the ships in a fleet during an engagement. Here he demonstrated not only the knowledge of surveying which he had acquired in Canada but also a flexibility of mind. This latter quality was not so apparent in his strictly political work. Unfortunately, constitutional problems could not be reduced to a set of symbols on a chart. During this period Cartwright served in the militia, despite his opposition to the American war, because of the danger of a French or Spanish invasion. It is another indication of the mildness of the official attitude that an outspoken critic should be allowed to retain his commission during this sensitive time.

In 1780 Major Cartwright finally married the patient Anne Dashwood. This self-effacing woman was to care for her husband with devotion until his death. The new Mrs Cartwright had little formal education and no ambition outside her family. She was undoubtedly typical of the wives of prominent men before the advent of feminism in being concerned with her domestic duties, with few distractions. Although childless, the marriage was a happy one. Cartwright's naturally pleasant disposition was a factor in the success of his marriage – his tendentiousness was not in evidence at his hearth – but his wife had a smooth, even temperament of her own. Especially in his later years it was a great comfort to Cartwright to have a generous partner to share his many disappointments and few triumphs.

A year after the Major's marriage his father died, leaving the estate of Marnham to the eldest son in the family. George Cartwright, having lost heavily in speculations in Labrador, wanted to divest himself of family affairs in order that he might return there. The Marnham estate was therefore sold at auction. By using all of his capital as well as borrowing money, John became its owner. For the next year he worked eleven hours a day to restore the prosperity of Marnham, which his father's business mismanagement and ill health had caused to deteriorate.[1] Marn-

[1] *Ibid.* p. 141.

ham was to be his home until 1788 when he sold it and bought an estate in Lincolnshire.

The labour which was necessary to restore Marnham cut into the Major's time for political activity; he wrote comparatively little during the decade after 1780. But his last substantial work for some time, published in 1780, the year of his marriage and the Gordon Riots, was a splendid example of pre-Painite radicalism. Entitled *The People's Barrier Against Undue Influence and Corruption: or the Commons House of Parliament According to the Constitution*, the book was an advance over *Take Your Choice!* in that it spelled out Cartwright's remedies in more detail and, if possible, even more confidently. Literal in his reading of history, uncritical of his sources, Cartwright could assert that Alfred the Great was a republican prince, at one time annual elections were held and all of the common people were represented in parliament, and that during this period England was prosperous and serene while art, commerce and charity flourished.[1] Here was his first excursion into the mythology of Anglo-Saxondom. But the happy situation which he described lasted during most of the Middle Ages, especially when the 'renowned Edwards' reigned, until the Forty Shilling Act of 1430 began that process of disenfranchisement which continued through Tudor and Stuart times.[2]

The constant historical and Biblical illusions – the assertions that England needed a restoration of her former liberties – mark this book as representative of a style of radical thought different from the iconoclasm of Paine's *The Rights of Man*. Cartwright did not talk about the dead hand of the past, nor did he discern a fundamental conflict between the rights of the living and the inhibitions imposed by our ancestors. Indeed, he gloried in England's heritage and sought to recover it by a restoration of past political practices. Yet in his refutation of the pretence that the king can do no harm and that ministers of the Crown are solely to blame, and in his flat and literal assertion that the king is the servant of the people[3] there is evidence of an astringent attitude which makes consistent his firm and unsentimental limita-

[1] *The People's Barrier* (London, 1780), pp. v, 10.

[2] *Ibid.* p. 31.

[3] *Ibid.* p. 48.

tions on the monarch's power. There were, said Cartwright, no such things as His Majesty's ministers, His Majesty's navy or His Majesty's revenues.[1] While Paine's form of republicanism was unappealing to him, Cartwright had little veneration for monarchy and noted that the word 'Republic' was used in former times to describe England's government.[2] In 1823, a year before he died, he noted cryptically that God makes men equal; kings make them unequal.[3] His love of the past centred around the image of an independent, arms bearing yeomanry meeting annually to cast their ballots for representatives in a sovereign parliament.

'I would to God that the people would cease to be victims of self-delusions; – that they would cease to attribute to the minister of the cabinet of the day all the sickness of the state, which has been diseased for ages...It is THEMSELVES that must seek the cure.'[4] While noting this fact, Cartwright also prescribed the remedy: 'natural reason and justice which abound in every honest mind...'.[5] For 'To be a MAN is, at all times and in all countries, a title to LIBERTY; and *he who doth not assert it deserves not the name of a* MAN!'[6] These principles should be expressed by universal male suffrage, annual parliaments and the secret ballot. Cartwright modified the scheme of representation stated in *Take Your Choice!* by proposing that each county elect representatives to the House of Commons in proportion to population. This would range from two for Rutland to forty-six for Yorkshire.[7] If a candidate for a district failed to present himself, a folkmote would be held to select men who must then run and serve if elected under penalty of law. Members would be paid and receive one shilling a mile for travelling expenses to and from London. In addition to the annual elections, members would be responsible to their constituents at folkmotes to be held on the last Thursday of May, at which time they must answer questions concerning their conduct in parliament.[8]

[1] *Ibid.* p. vii.
[2] *Ibid.* p. vi.
[3] *The English Constitution Produced and Illustrated* (London, 1823), p. 231.
[4] *The People's Barrier*, etc., p. 9.
[5] *Ibid.* p. 10.
[6] *Ibid.* p. 29.
[7] *Ibid.* pp. 94–5. Under this scheme Scotland would continue to be under-represented with only 45 out of 558 members.
[8] *Ibid.* pp. 102–4, 109.

The honesty and rationality of this method was self-evident to Cartwright. Although he acknowledged that there was little popular demand for a freely elected parliament the people must want it for they desired that the ills of the country be cured, and for this an independent parliament was necessary. Therefore he claimed to speak for the majority in demanding annual parliaments and equal representation. The dilemma of radical minorities in all ages was faced by Cartwright with all the confidence of Jean Jacques Rousseau. 'Upon what is SELF-EVIDENT, upon what is unanswerably DEMONSTRATED, upon what is undeniably JUST, there can be no diversity of opinion', noted Cartwright.[1] He went even further in claiming that acts of parliament, if corrupt, are not legally binding – that people have the constitutional right to ignore parliament if it forbids them to take the law into their own hands. This is because each House of Commons is responsible to the people who elected it and when it expires all its rights and powers revert to the people. Each new parliament may do as it pleases without being bound by the acts of its predecessors. Thomas Paine's notion of clear and separate generations was not only anticipated but exceeded by Cartwright in these few pages.[2]

It is very doubtful whether Cartwright understood all the implications of this doctrine. He was certainly no Jacobin and usually demonstrated a veneration for old institutions and customs. Indeed, one of his weaknesses was seeing a continuity in parliamentary practice that was not always there. Literal-minded, he sometimes fell into the trap of which Collingwood warned us: thinking that we understand the thoughts of past writers merely because we possess their words. Furthermore, *The People's Barrier* was primarily an attack on the corruption of the House of Commons in the eighteenth century. Its proposed remedies, annual elections and universal male suffrage, were ancient practices intended to reconstruct that which was essentially sound rather than to build a new constitution. Cartwright's exaggerated respect for the efficacy of reason (and of human beings' willingness to employ it) led him into the inconsistency

[1] *Ibid.* p. 89.

[2] *Ibid.* pp. 78–82.

of countenancing a radical extremism of which he was bound to disapprove were it ever practised.

The People's Barrier reminds us constantly of the real villains in the country who have caused England to be overwhelmed

> with a debt of near *two hundred millions*, mortgaged almost beyond redemption, still farther distressed by the daily decay of its manufactures and the cutting off [sic] its sources of wealth, and at the same time dishonoured in its arms, sacrificed to the rapacity of blood-suckers in a thousand shapes, and finally mocked and insulted by the tyrant faction *which governs, as Walpole did*, by *votes bought with the people's own money*, with a total denial of any accounts which can enable the people to discover whether their affairs have been managed with fidelity or with treachery.[1]

Cartwright sometimes seemed to be divorced from economic questions but his early writings bear witness to the resentment of a man who felt that government had fallen into the hands of strange, commercial forces and that it must be rescued. He would have denied any prejudice against commerce *per se* and his later actions on behalf of his brother indicate that he viewed honest manufacturing favourably; it was money power which had to be crushed.

A clue to Cartwright's state of mind was provided the following year in a lengthy pamphlet entitled *Letter to the Deputies of the Associated and Petitioning Counties, Cities and Towns; on the means necessary to a Reformation of Parliament.* The thesis of this little known work is that the English people must be awakened politically to the need for massive reform; half-way measures would not suffice. The familiar themes of universal suffrage and annual parliaments were stressed but there was a note of urgency that was missing from *Take Your Choice!* and *The People's Barrier*. Ratepayer suffrage, triennial parliaments and fiscal reform were seen as expedients ('it would be pulling up straws when we ought to be securing the harvest')[2] and the people were urged not to pay taxes until they were fully represented.[3] This early unwillingness to compromise on basic principles of reform was at the time a deeply held characteristic, although later on Cart-

[1] *Ibid.* p. 46.

[2] *Letters to the Deputies*, etc. (London, 1781), p. 27. Also, pp. 9–10, 20, 26.

[3] *Ibid.* p. 42.

wright would work with individuals who had less thoroughgoing views of the amount of reform which England needed. The *Letter to the Deputies*, which was clearly written in haste, was Cartwright's response to his colleagues in reform who were willing to settle for a tinkering with political and financial institutions.

Nevertheless, as late as the spring of 1782, Cartwright was optimistic about the possibility of securing the type of reform he desired, although on the Westminster Committee the Rockingham faction had acted as a roadblock to radical measures. *Give us our Rights!* took up the subject at length for the last time in many years. The thesis of the pamphlet was that king and nobility excepted, the rest of the nation consisted of the commoners, whose organ was the House of Commons. A complete and equally proportional representation in that House was their right. The last words were 'a *minority* of the commons of England have no right to appoint legislators and tax-masters over the *majority*'.[1] While restating his usual request and urging that the Septennial Act and the Forty Shilling Act of 1430 be 'cast into the flames', Cartwright made clear both his respect for English history and his real desire for more economical and honest government. Still, economy and honesty were not his main objectives.

Give us our Rights! was really an attack upon Edmund Burke and his belief that the House of Commons could act as the people's trustee. There are no trustees for the people except the people themselves, said Cartwright.[2] In this pamphlet he criticized virtual representation and again made clear that his own concern was popular participation in government and not a moderate reform of existing abuses. *Letter to the Deputies* and *Give us our Rights!* indicate that in 1781 and early 1782 Cartwright was still hopeful of the possibility of political change but also that he had become aware that some of his partners in reform were not going to pursue this goal to the extent which he wanted. *Give us our Rights!* was dated 23 March 1782, only three days

[1] *Give us our Rights!* (London, n.d.). The pamphlet is dated 23 March 1782 and inscribed to Jebb, Loftt and Sharp. See pages 46 and 56.

[2] *Ibid.* pp. 24–6.

after Rockingham succeeded North as chief minister and brought Shelburne, Fox, Sheridan and Burke into office with him. With good reason, Cartwright did not expect much from this ministry. Yet Burke's economical reforms were not contemptible when viewed in the long range of British history. They could scarcely be expected to win the complete commendation, however, of the thoroughgoing Cartwright, whose purpose in writing the pamphlet was to bestir the people into activity which would end stagnation in political life.

Although the next few years witnessed Cartwright's participation in numerous petitions and meetings, nothing came of this activity. Petitions may indeed have bombarded parliament but they were futile. *Haute politique* centring around the king and the leaders of political factions made a mockery of all this earnest effort. Besides, in 1783, the peak year for petitions, only one-tenth of the British electorate demanded reform.[1] Cartwright sat in the House of Commons visitors gallery and listened with enthusiasm to Pitt's famous speech of April 1785 in which the Prime Minister advanced for the last time a proposal for parliamentary reform. The scheme failed, despite Pitt's zealous advocacy, which extended to summoning his friend Wilberforce from the Riviera to cast his vote in favour of it. The hope of fundamental political reform thus died in England many years before the outbreak of the French Revolution and perhaps as early as 1782. Cartwright was disappointed but did not give up hope.

By the early 1780s Cartwright had clearly stepped across the threshold of his career. He was an important figure among the small band of radical reformers and was known to the fairly considerable, but amorphous group which desired mild change in the political system. Despite his shortcomings as a thinker, he was accepted by well educated, highly intelligent men such as Capell Lofft and John Jebb. Demands for moderate reform would soon evaporate under the intense heat generated by the French Revolution, but even before this it had gradually become clear that little could be expected in the way of political change beyond some

[1] Christie, *Wilkes, Wyvill and Reform*, p. 184.

measures to reduce the amount of funds and offices available to the Crown for bribery and patronage. Much of the reform movement had been aroused by disgust over the ineptitude of the government in its handling of the American crisis. When this mood, which reached its peak from 1780 to 1782, faded, so did the cause of reform. Cartwright and his colleagues were left stranded.

CHAPTER 3

THE FRENCH REVOLUTION AND ENGLISH REFORM

The late 1780s saw the cause of reform at a low ebb and Cartwright busy with private matters. He and his wife adopted the six-year-old daughter of his brother Edmund, the inventor of the power loom, whose own wife had died in 1786. This arrangement caused less comment in the eighteenth century than it would today. The kindly couple could provide a more tranquil home than Edmund, and for her part, Frances Dorothy repaid her new parents with devotion. In 1826 she published the only biography of John and seldom can anyone have had a less critical and more dedicated admirer narrate the course of a career which was, more often than not, bound in shallows. In 1788, Cartwright lost heavily in a speculation involving a spinning mill for wool, but in the same year he was fortunate enough to buy a large estate at Brothertoft, near Boston, in Lincolnshire. The principal crop of this new farm was woad, used for dyeing, and the substantial profits financed his activities in the field of reform.[1]

While Cartwright was busy with these personal affairs, John Jebb died. Jebb was perhaps the most talented of the radical leaders; he was certainly the one with the broadest views. Few of his colleagues possessed the flexibility of mind to associate reform of the universities and the legal and prison systems with their schemes for political purity. Although he was unusually far-seeing, nevertheless, Jebb did have that stubborn, doctrinaire quality which marked radicals at the time. Even if Jebb had lived, he and the other members of the Society for Constitutional Information could not have brought about the reform which they desired. This was in part due to their dogmatism which made for inflexible political tactics. Captivated by theory, the radicals

[1] Cartwright took the initiative in forming a cartel with his fellow woad growers to fix prices, wages, and the amount of production for their mutual advantage. *L and C*, vol. 1, pp. 177–8. His niece, who suppressed some information about him, included this fact in her biography.

were all wretched practical politicians. Yet supposing an alliance could have been cemented with the middle-of-the-road Whig reformers, it is doubtful that much could have been achieved once the resentment throughout the country over the mishandling of the American war began to fade. The times were not propitious for a reform movement of the middle and upper classes and no one wanted to make common cause with the lower orders.

At this point, let us imagine a reformer with wide human sympathies combined with a gift for seizing new initiatives. Recognizing that the traditional political and religious appeals met with only a limited response, he would have extended the programme for reform to include social and economic aims and sought to foster the political consciousness of the almost unrepresented workers of the country. The SCI, for example, with all its talk of 'the people' was not really moved by the problems of the working classes and, except for Cartwright, did not believe that every man should vote. Cartwright himself lacked the vision to associate the working classes with the reform movement and at this time was so busy with personal matters that he rarely attended meetings of the SCI. Here was an opportunity for someone to articulate the grievances of the huge but completely unorganized mass of the population and to present a wide-ranging programme of change that would include reform of parliament. The individual who could have done this perhaps did not exist and radical politics continued to be divorced from social and economic life. The power brokers in parliament well understood the connection between political and material interests, but their actions caused the reformers to react in an abstract, unrealistic fashion and to look backward, not forward.[1]

The effect of an alliance between the radicals and the common people would not have been to ensure immediate reform, but it would have clarified discontent and pointed the way toward a

[1] The belief that practical politics are sordid persisted among radicals. Two of Cartwright's later associates, William Cobbett and Henry Hunt, cut sorry figures when they were finally elected to parliament and Cobbett had early decided that party politics must be abolished. See John W. Osborne, *William Cobbett: His Thought and His Times* (New Brunswick, 1966), ch. v. A later tribune of the people, Robert Blatchford, arrived at the same conclusion. See Laurence Thompson, *Robert Blatchford: Portrait of an Englishman* (London, 1951), pp. 52–5.

more effective political structure in which those advocating change and those wanting the preservation of the *status quo* would have been more sharply defined. But in 1789 all forms of political activity were disrupted. The French Revolution began when Cartwright was almost totally absorbed in his new estate at Brothertoft. He was in occasional correspondence with other reformers but had given up writing for publication. Like most other political observers, Cartwright's initial impression of events across the Channel was favourable; unlike some radicals, disillusion gradually took hold of his mind. All was still sweetness and light in August 1789 when he addressed a letter to the President of the Committee of Constitution of the Estates General, congratulating the French but warning them also to hold frequent elections to preserve their new freedom. At this time Cartwright shared the widespread assumption that the French were emulating the English practice of a constitutional monarchy.[1] When King Louis XVI was executed in 1793, Cartwright condemned the action and saw it as the work of 'the demagogues of an ignorant rabble'.[2]

The feeling of enthusiasm for the Revolution which had affected most Englishmen of substance soon dissipated under the impact of events. As its violent and expansionist tendencies developed, many considered that Edmund Burke had been right when he condemned the Revolution from the start. Burke's veneration of established institutions was so strong that he was called the Bossuet of politics, but he was no narrow reactionary and in the mid-1780s had sponsored several measures of political reform. Yet he was opposed to any organic change in the constitution and throughout his career condemned making venerable practices the subject of rational speculation. With his love for the Anglo-Saxon and medieval English constitution, Cartwright shared with Burke a belief in the validity of the past. Both men disliked Jacobinism, with its call for beginning political life anew. But Cartwright's mind was not mystical and, unlike Burke, he could not venerate what he could not comprehend. He liked the old English constitution because he thought that he could under-

[1] *L and C*, vol. 1, pp. 182–5.

[2] *Ibid.* p. 195.

stand it and because it had worked, not merely because it was old. It would be foolish to belabour a comparison of the minds of these two unequal men, but it is worth noting that both the great conservative and this representative of an important strand of radical thought distrusted the free and unhampered play of ideas. In this they were like the great majority of their countrymen, whose practical common sense warned them of the danger of metaphysics when it was applied to politics.

The political climate of the early 1790s was not favourable to reform and all the tactical skill of the radicals could not have brought them success at this time. Underlining this fact and of significance for future political developments, was the agreement on another issue between the instinctive conservatism of Burke and Cartwright's own form of radicalism.[1] Neither man liked or trusted the great intellectual movement of the eighteenth century which we today call the Enlightenment, though in a few subtle ways Cartwright was influenced by it. In Cartwright's case the Enlightenment had little appeal because of his ignorance of foreign languages and history and his distrust of the French. His dry mind saw no need of foreign examples. Like his colleagues in the SCI, Cartwright's inspiration came from English experience and they were all indebted, more than many of them realized, to the political thought of the seventeenth century. Thomas Paine, whose ideas were shortly to explode on the political scene, was not a figure in this English tradition and his ruthless dissection of the past was as foreign (and, therefore, suspect) as the cosmopolitanism of Paine's personal life.

Painite radicalism was much more thoroughgoing than that of the SCI and over 200,000 copies of *The Rights of Man*, which circulated in the country in the 1790s, testified to an interest in the new Jacobinism. Iconoclastic toward traditional institutions such as king, aristocracy and church hierarchy, Paine also enormously

[1] Cartwright had sent Burke a copy of *Take Your Choice!*, but he persistently underestimated the devotion of the Rockingham faction to the aristocratic constitution as it had been developed in the seventeenth century. See Carl Cone, *Burke and the Nature of Politics: The Age of the American Revolution* (Lexington, Ky., 1957), p. 293. Undoubtedly the failure of the Rockingham faction to embrace 'real' reform contributed to his disillusionment with political parties.

broadened radical proposals for change to include a progressive income tax, old-age pensions, government allowances to families with children, national support of education and public works projects. This was 'radical reform' with a vengeance. Republicanism was bad enough but when it was linked to the germ of the welfare state a shudder went through the ranks of the propertied classes. A new basis for political reform had been provided by the genius of Paine and radicalism had reached a turning-point which it stubbornly refused to recognize.

The anonymous author of *The Jockey Club*, a series of satirical sketches of prominent personalities, typified those Englishmen who saw the French Revolution as good. Like many radical intellectuals he considered that nothing in his own country was right; the enemy, on the other hand, could do no wrong. Such a view would be too much for Cartwright's common sense to endure. Nevertheless, in the Painite *Jockey Club* there were several similarities of views with those of the Major: an emphasis upon honesty in government, a dislike of lawyers, and a belief that government was a science.[1] All of this was orthodox radical doctrine. The absence of any coordinated efforts – anything which resembled a 'movement' – made each group work in isolation and a feature of radical writing at the time was its tendency to ignore the work of others who were engaged in the same general struggle.

From Fox downwards the leaders of reform hastened to dissociate themselves from Paine's ideas and Cartwright himself proposed a resolution reaffirming the established constitutional structure at a meeting of the Society of the Friends of the People on 9 May 1792.[2] Despite its title, this group was aloof from the people and critical of Paine and his ideas, although it was willing to accept ratepayer suffrage in the boroughs and single-member county constituencies. High dues and admissions procedures similar to those of an exclusive private club kept membership low. When Cartwright was accepted, five members resigned. The Society of the Friends of the People did protest the political

[1] *The Jockey Club*, etc. Part 1 (2nd ed.) (London, 1792), pp. 41–3.

[2] *L and C*, vol. 1, p. 192 and Cone, *The English Jacobins*, p. 100.

repression of the mid-1790s, but its ambivalence toward reform typified the dilemma of radicalism.

There were two reasons for this dilemma. The first concerned Paine, whose Deism and praise of violent overthrow of government, as well as his levelling doctrines, embarrassed moderate reformers and left the cause of radical change more vulnerable to conservative attack. The rapid emergence of Paine as the outstanding radical spokesman also facilitated a mood of extreme reaction which had begun with the general disillusionment over the French Revolution. Thus, in addition to Paine's exuberant proposals for sweeping alteration, reformers of the stamp of Cartwright had to bear the burden of an increasingly violent chain of events in France. Conservatives pointed out that what was now abhorrent in that country had begun with requests for moderate reform. It proved easy for them to denounce their opponents as both Jacobin and un-English. The radicals were not able to avoid these slanders, which clung to them for two or three decades to come. They never succeeded in overcoming their dilemma; tacks to both the political right and the political left failed to win them substantial support.

Moderate and thoroughly English, most reformers could not counterattack with any vigour and seemed on the defensive. Some, like Fox, reacted to events in France in the genial, tolerant spirit of the eighteenth century. Unable to grasp the brand new nature of the struggle with its violent nationalism and foretaste of total war, they persisted in seeing good in their country's mortal enemy. At home, the SCI, after some embarrassed hesitation, declined Paine's offer of £1,000 from the royalties of *The Rights of Man*, asserting that Paine deserved to keep the money himself.[1] But Paine, like Robespierre (or Lenin) was incorruptible and the incident served to illustrate the fact that political initiative was being taken away from the moderates by extremists. In the general repression of the mid-1790s anyone who proposed change was liable to be charged with treason, and the government did not draw fine distinctions.

As early as 1791, even before England and France went to war,

[1] Cone, *The English Jacobins*, p. 105.

Cartwright began to feel the heat of discrimination. After attending a meeting to celebrate the second anniversary of the fall of the Bastille, he was advised by the Duke of Newcastle that promotion to the vacant lieutenant-colonelcy of his regiment would not be forthcoming. Newcastle, as Lord-Lieutenant of Nottinghamshire, made it clear that Cartwright's political opinions were the obstacle to this elevation. Although it was not the first time that he had been passed over, Cartwright refused to resign his commission and not until the following year was he deprived of it. Cartwright did not accept the second insult mildly and the depth of his resentment may be seen in *A Letter to the Duke of Newcastle*, which was written in 1792. One hundred and twelve pages were spent in detailing Cartwright's side of the controversy and then, as though his bitterness had not been satisfied, there was a postscript of forty-five more pages. In this very long 'letter' Cartwright displayed more personal animosity than appears in any of his other writings, and he roundly denounced Newcastle's conduct as 'illiberal, dishonourable, and unconstitutional'.[1] Cartwright's discharge from his regiment was probably the severest blow which he had to accept as a consequence of his political opinions, worse than his failure to be elected to parliament. Others, less lucky, were in danger of losing their lives.

The pace of reaction was quickening and in 1793 Cartwright publicly complained of encroachments by the Crown upon the people's liberty.[2] This open letter stated the position of those radicals who were not followers of Paine. It defended the radical political programme, but persons who demanded an equal division of property were ridiculed and the government was assured that the best way to halt the spread of republicanism was to grant political reform.[3] The encroachment of the Crown upon the people's liberty and the control by the nobility of many seats in the House of Commons were the real dangers to liberty. Turning to foreign affairs, Cartwright roundly condemned the

[1] *A Letter to the Duke of Newcastle* (London, 1792), passim. The *Letter* adds little to what we know of Cartwright's political views. The Duke's action was certainly illiberal and probably dishonourable as well, but not, strictly speaking, unconstitutional.

[2] *A Letter from John Cartwright Esq. to a Friend at Boston in the County of Lincoln*, p. 7.

[3] *Ibid.* pp. 17–24.

Continental despotisms and praised the United States of America, while blaming Pitt for involving the country in war against France.[1] The latter charge became an article of faith for radicals in subsequent years. Reform of abuses in a fundamentally sound constitution was his goal. At this time, as in the decade after Waterloo, Cartwright staked out a position among those whose desire for change stopped short of a revolution. Cobbett's famous slogan of a generation later, 'We want great alteration, but we want nothing new', was anticipated here.

Much of this pamphlet, however, was an attack upon Loyal Associations which were beginning to defend church and state against 'Jacobinism'. These zealous defenders of the *status quo* made life miserable for anyone suspected of harbouring disloyal views, and the moderate reformers were included with those holding violent revolutionary tendencies.[2] Such people were not likely to be reassured by Cartwright's assertions that the House of Commons belonged to the people or his rhetorical question, 'Has any peer, because a particular old ruined castle is upon his estate, a right to as many votes as fifty, an hundred, or two hundred of his brethren?'[3] Also, his attacks upon levellers might seem to be trimming. The dispute of the 1770s and 1780s was becoming rancorous and dangerous.

For its part, the government made little effort to distinguish between the various groups of radicals, but responded with a harsh policy of repression. Proclamations were issued against publications deemed seditious and in 1794 the *habeas corpus* act was suspended. The net was further tightened in the following year when two acts of parliament made reform agitation in effect impossible. The first extended the law against treason to include virtually any discussion of constitutional grievances. The second act limited the size of public meetings to fifty persons and gave the magistrates wide discretionary powers to regulate such meetings. Both acts were for a term of three years. As early as 1793 several savage sentences of transportation were inflicted upon

[1] *Ibid.* p. 36.

[2] Black, *The Association*, discusses these groups and their techniques of stifling dissent.

[3] *A Letter*, etc., pp. 38–9.

reformers in Scotland. Cartwright unsuccessfully sought to intercede for a revision of the sentences. All prior promises of reform by Pitt were ignored as the government concentrated entirely upon that policy of victory over revolutionary France which, to his admirers, was Pitt's chief claim to glory. The mood of reaction spread to the people. 'Church and king' mobs, composed of all classes, caused terror among any who desired change. These well organized Loyal Associations subordinated themselves to magistrates in the cause of suppression. Declared reformers were in danger of arrest or physical violence. Some fled the country; others performed acts of what would later be described as 'inner emigration' and left the field of reform.

Since Cartwright was intimately connected with the cause of reform, he was in personal danger. He attended the state trials of 1794 and testified on behalf of Horne Tooke, one of those accused of high treason.[1] Such a serious charge could only be sustained if the government could prove that the accused had plotted to use force. Thus Cartwright's testimony was dedicated to demonstrating the pacific and moderate nature of the reform with which he and Tooke were associated.[2] The government had attempted more than it could prove. The calm behaviour of the defendants and inspired defence of their advocate, Erskine, helped to win verdicts of acquittal. Had convictions been secured, there can be no doubt that next time the net was cast Cartwright would have been caught. Quite likely only Cartwright's absorption in his private affairs had prevented him from being associated in the call for a national convention which had led to the arrest of his colleagues.

Even so, he was involved in one tragedy. Daniel Holt, a young Newark printer, was tried and sentenced to four years' imprisonment in Newgate plus a heavy fine for publishing a short article by Cartwright that was written in 1782. The imprisonment

[1] John Horne Tooke (1736–1821), clergyman and philologist, was a moderate radical whose views were similar to Cartwright's in that they emphasized England's ancient political liberties and eschewed Paine's Jacobinism. He was responsible for a permanent change in the constitution: in 1801, after being elected to parliament, his colleagues responded by declaring clergymen ineligible to serve in the House of Commons.

[2] *L and C*, vol. 1, pp. 214–19.

probably hastened Holt's early death. Cartwright felt the situation deeply, although he had no prior knowledge of Holt's intention to republish the article and was in no way responsible for the sentence. He appeared at the trial but his proferred testimony was rejected as inadmissible. Under the broad law of seditious libel anyone involved in the process of publication might be accused, printers and distributors as well as authors and publishers. Cartwright's evidence failed to show that Holt did not print the offending article, and for that reason it was rejected.[1] When a free press did emerge in England in the 1830s it was because courageous men had risked health and fortune in combating government oppression over issues like this one.

The tempo of reaction continued to increase. As noted, two acts were passed which were aimed at treasonable practices and seditious meetings. The sponsors, Pitt and Grenville, interpreted the scope of these crimes in the broadest possible terms. The Treasonable Practices Act made those who published criticism of the king or of the constitution liable to transportation for seven years. The Seditious Meetings Act prohibited for the next three years meetings of more than fifty people, except with the permission of local magistrates, who might dissolve meetings and arrest the speaker at any time. Some Whigs and Radicals made common cause in opposition to these acts, Fox being particularly eloquent in parliament and Wyvill emerging from his retirement.[2] Despite ill health Cartwright addressed himself to the growing political repression. His contribution to the protest was *A Letter to the High Sheriff of the County of Lincoln*. In it he took his familiar line that it was not the reformers who were trying to overthrow the constitution but those who held office through bribery and corruption. The discontent of the reformers was justified since it sought to achieve equal representation.[3] An accompanying petition was rejected by the sheriff without being read to the county meeting.[4]

As the mood of conservatism grew, it enveloped some men

[1] *Ibid.* pp. 199–202.

[2] P. A. Brown, *The French Revolution in English History* (London, 1965), p. 152; H. W. C. Davis, *The Age of Grey and Peel* (Oxford, 1964), p. 46.

[3] *A Letter*, etc. (London, 1795), passim.

[4] *L and C*, vol. I, p. 231.

who only a few years before were considered to have advanced views. One of these was the famous writer on agriculture, Arthur Young. Despite his trenchant criticism of the weaknesses of the old regime in France, Young had adopted an extreme Tory position toward the great revolution and was fond of labelling English reformers as 'Jacobin'. Since 1793 he had been Secretary to the newly-formed Board of Agriculture where he was able to see that some of his theories about soil cultivation were put to good use. Young was fully aware that he had become a prophet honoured in his own country and was harsh to dissidents. Cartwright's other publication of 1795, a pamphlet entitled *The Commonwealth in Danger*, was provoked by Young's attacks.

The Commonwealth in Danger (1795) did more than deplore Young's politics and reemphasize Cartwright's general theme of mass public participation in politics. While making clear Cartwright's dislike of Robespierre, the document pointed out the French heritage of despotism, priesthood and superstition, so different from that of England. *The Commonwealth in Danger* urged a generous policy toward France.[1] Apart from a brief reference to the desirability of the gradual emancipation of slaves in the Empire, the document is significant for two assertions. The first was that the British government had been basically a Republic or Commonwealth and must regain this state by reform.[2] This went beyond his vague reference to a Republic in *The People's Barrier*. In this case he was arguing against a repressive oligarchy rather than King George III, but he was certainly influenced by the writings of Paine and the success of the United States of America. The second theme was to echo frequently in Cartwright's future writings. It was that of a militia composed of citizens who would both vote and protect the country.[3]

This scheme may be seen as a reflection of the growing impersonality of English society created by commercialization and urbanization. Individual landowners in America, like George Washington, might be compared to Cincinnatus, called away

[1] *The Commonwealth in Danger* (London, 1795), pp. 19, 34, 50. Cartwright naively thought that the French could be won over to friendship by English concessions concerning trade.

[2] *Ibid.* p. 97.

[3] *Ibid.* p. 15.

from the plough to defend his country; the image was absurd in late eighteenth-century England. Few institutions are as prone to attack by persons who feel themselves overwhelmed by a complex society as is a standing army. The locally based militia would be, as Cartwright sensed, a means of providing a community of feeling in which every man could see the results of his contributions. Thus, the desire to revert to a militia on the Anglo-Saxon model was produced by more than a war of which the Major disapproved. The idea would eventually become one of the most salient features of any Cartwright book or article and be linked firmly with political reform.[1]

An assumption that a Republican form of government was best for the country was held by many members of the London Corresponding Society, which had been formed by a shoemaker, Thomas Hardy, in 1792. An entrance fee of one shilling and a penny a week dues opened this organization to the working class. It was thus the most democratic of all the reform organizations. The LCS had the usual radical platform of universal male suffrage, annual elections and a reduction of government expenditure. There was no programme of social or economic reform, but a number of the members joined because of discontent arising from low wages or unemployment. Members of the LCS kept in touch with similar organizations in the provinces and were exceptionally prominent among the victims of government repression during the State Trials of the mid-1790s. Overtures toward the Society of the Friends of the People were not reciprocated by this elitist brand of reformers, and the LCS languished after 1795 and was banned by the government in 1799. Although Paine's ideas were influential, members of the LCS generally had little education, and were so thoroughly English that only one year before being suppressed they debated a motion to form a loyal corps to resist a possible French invasion.[2]

Despite similar goals Cartwright had no connection with the LCS, but belonged to the more reputable SCI and Society of the

[1] A similar attitude in favour of a militia and against the standing army appeared in Bolingbroke's *The Craftsman*. See Kramnick, *Bolingbroke*, pp. 72–3.

[2] J. S. Watson, *The Age of George III* (Oxford, 1960), p. 361.

Friends of the People and carried on correspondence with influential figures such as Fox. It was Cartwright's claim that he would work with anyone who sought constitutional reform by legal means, but he was really very particular about whom he associated with in this cause. Although he was later associated with the Hampden Club movement, throughout his career he preferred respectable men of property, such as himself, to provide the leadership of any reform body. Cartwright was never a popular political general; there existed not the slightest touch of charisma about him. At the end of his career he was well respected, but primarily because of his decades of devotion to reform. Illness and pressing personal affairs diverted his attention during the crucial mid-1790s when freedom was on trial in Great Britain, but it would be unwise to assume that if Cartwright had been able to participate fully he would have been ready to embrace the role of a crowd pleaser.

Repression of dissent was reaching its peak in 1796 with some reformers in jail or transported overseas and others about to go into hiding. John Thelwall, an enthusiastic advocate of the principles of the French Revolution who had already been tried for treason in 1794,[1] was meeting no success in his missionary tours on behalf of radical reform. Sailors broke up a meeting at Great Yarmouth and Loyal Associations persecuted him everywhere he went.[2] At this juncture Cartwright produced another lengthy pamphlet, which was originally intended to be a speech which ill health prevented him from giving. Uncompromising in its attack upon political evils as Cartwright saw them, the pamphlet was also noteworthy for its being divorced from both the specific issue of government policy toward dissent and current economic problems.

All reformers during this period were cautious about falling foul of the law; Cartwright made practically no reference to current events but wrote in general principles. Also, there was no reference in his writings to the terrible economic suffering which followed a series of bad harvests and led to the Speenhamland

[1] He was acquitted, along with Horne Tooke.

[2] Brown, *French Revolution*, pp. 152–3.

System, begun in the preceding year in Berkshire and endorsed by an act of parliament in 1796. The Speenhamland System permitted wages to be supplemented from local taxes depending upon the price of bread and the size of the family. It was a desperation measure which prevented outright starvation but did nothing to prevent poverty and was scrapped ten years after Cartwright's death. Cartwright deplored high taxes but made no connection between them and basic economic conditions which affected the common people. It was another example of his failure to relate political and economic issues.

Cartwright's pamphlet, called *The Constitutional Defence of England*, addressed to the freeholders of the county of Lincoln, courageously attacked the system of representation, political repression and the war with France, which he referred to as 'The Rotten Borough War'.[1] The fact that it was France, not England, which had declared war was being forgotten within the ranks of the radicals. Although he asserted that he had no quarrel with the king or the nobility, but only with the former's advisers and the boroughmongers,[2] his complaints indicated otherwise. In addition to beginning the war against France and levying high taxes, the peers' control of the election of 150 members of the House of Commons was a violation of the Constitution, especially because the members of the upper house were not selected for reasons of talent, experience or public virtue but because of their birth.[3] As for the king, he was the vassal of the parliament, which controlled his money.[4] Cartwright's remedies were annual elections to the House of Commons to counterbalance the weight of the peers. The free choice of representatives (by secret ballot) was necessary since, as he observed, wisdom, knowledge and virtue are not hereditary qualities.[5] These were strong words, written when the radicals were in disarray and they placed Cartwright in some danger.

The integrity of elections against the pressure of boroughmonger peers was a theme of *The Constitutional Defence of*

[1] *The Constitutional Defence of England* (London, 1796), passim. See especially p. 69 and pp. 97–9 for his blame of the government for 'plunging' England into war.

[2] *Ibid.* p. 65.

[3] *Ibid.* pp. 16, 21.

[4] *Ibid.* p. 55.

[5] *Ibid.* pp. 114ff.

England. The same idea was also featured in Cartwright's negotiations which were aimed at securing nomination as a candidate from Boston at the general election of 1796. He professed himself willing to serve for just one year and without pay, but he would not campaign and demanded the seat in an uncontested election. Consistent with his call in *The Constitutional Defence of England* for a popularly chosen House of Commons to counterbalance the influence of hereditary legislators in the upper house, he avowed the disinterested nature of his offer and the importance of incorruptible candidates who had been freely selected.[1] Boston was a borough whose electorate of about two hundred was well (and profitably) acquainted with methods of bribery. It was perhaps no surprise to Cartwright that his candidacy was never properly started.

By this time the cause of reform was not prospering. The 1794 State Trials had frightened the middle class and later there was a feeling among the public that radicalism was in some way connected with the naval mutinies of 1797 and even the rebellion of the United Irishmen in the following year. There were grounds for this suspicion, but they too often provided merely an excuse for inaction. To propose alteration of the established political institutions was a risky venture. The Fox–Grey resolutions of 1797, which called for triennial parliaments, a uniform household franchise for boroughs and the elimination of some of the more corrupt seats in the lower house, were rejected in the House of Commons by a vote of 256 to 91. The friends of Fox therefore seceded from both houses of parliament and many normally active private citizens of liberal persuasion followed their example by refusing to continue their interest in politics. A good deal of political activity was almost suspended for the duration of the war as England settled down to what was to prove a long struggle.

John Thelwall, who, as we have seen, had been arrested by the government but declared not guilty of treason by a jury in 1794, was one of those who retired into private life. So did the radical tailor, Francis Place. Thelwall contented himself with becoming an obscure teacher of elocution; Place devoted his energies to

[1] *L and C*, vol. 1, pp. 235–9.

building up his business before returning to politics at what was judged a more auspicious time. Arrests of minor figures for trivial offences continued to occur. The disappearance of the SCI after May 1794 was a better illustration of the situation than the pique of the Foxites or the fears of the radical Thelwall. The rank and file of the SCI were solid middle-class citizens who were committed to the type of reform with which Cartwright was associated. It has been noted that the end of the SCI (the society was never formally dissolved but simply failed to continue its meetings) was the end of a phase of English thought that had begun with the Levellers.[1] Other groups may have taken up the challenge but they were from a lower social stratum, had little money or power and were politically suspect as being Jacobin. The reneging of the middle class deprived the cause of reform of whatever respectability it may have enjoyed.

Minor as Cartwright's role was, it was symptomatic of what had occurred. It was representative of an old-fashioned radicalism that was not harmonious with Jacobinism or with the economically motivated doctrines of the following century. Cartwright was bound in his social and economic views by the conventions of his age. For example, in 1791, vexed by the rioting of farm labourers in Lincolnshire who had combined to protest the use of poor Irish harvest workers, he wrote and distributed gratis a pamphlet entitled *Plain Truths for Plain Men, by a Holland Fen-Farmer*. The contents are illustrative.

One musket and one bayonet in defence of peace and law, is a match for a score of scythes in the hands of men conscious of criminality. When each farmer is known to have arms for himself, and for two, or three, or more trusty persons, and all are ready on the least alarm to defend themselves and neighbours, there will be no bullying any one out of the profits of his harvest, and the idea of mob-law will become ridiculous.

Riots, my friends, are a disgrace to any country inhabited by civilized men, originating in the folly and wickedness of a few lawless persons; their beginnings are small, but who can tell where they will end? And who can restore to the community property once destroyed, or lives once lost.[2]

[1] Cone, *English Jacobins*, p. 213. As Brown notes, the repression was supported by 'public opinion' (*French Revolution*, p. 160), though this force was still confined largely to those with a property stake in society.

[2] *L and C*, vol. 1, pp. 186–7.

Where property was at stake, Cartwright could be as zealous for law and order as he was ardent for liberty when abstract constitutional doctrines were concerned.

At the beginning of this chapter a reform programme which would have included economic and social change was mentioned. It was beyond the capacity of anyone to have it effected during the decades of the 1780s and 1790s. More important, the wide spectrum of the political reform movement, which ranged from the Friends of the People through the Society for Constitutional Information to the various corresponding societies, did not realize that it was proposing old remedies for a new situation. Cartwright may be placed on the left wing of the SCI but his belief in an unalloyed universal manhood suffrage loses some of its impact when we realize that he did not believe that the social order would alter much after this principle had been enacted. It is also necessary to recognize that he did not grasp the instrumental nature of the ballot: that the people would not be content merely to vote with a view of restoring an ancient constitution, but would use their power to provide for their material needs. Some of the conservatives who rejected any suggestion of reform may have had a truer understanding of the possibilities of an extension of the suffrage than most advocates of change. Cartwright himself certainly would not have been as enthusiastic for reform if he could have foreseen its consequences.

Cartwright's problem was a lack of vision, not hypocrisy. His was a mind which was dominated by political ideas to such an extent that it was closed to any others. This was a failing which was common to most writers on this subject. Three great political revolutions, English, American and French, exercised an immense fascination over them. Whether one's attitude toward them was approval or horror was less important than the preoccupation with the technique of governing. Paine and perhaps a few of the lesser radicals grasped some of the broad consequences which were liable to flow from a major political change; they knew that politics was not divorced from society. These were the men who were in greatest danger from the government. To do Cartwright and his fellow members of the SCI justice, they were well aware of the possibility of entrenched political interests furthering their material ambitions, but they detested this practice, struggled against it and hoped to replace it by a return to an imaginary Eden in which politics was unsullied by sordid considerations and the ordinary individual could live almost without being aware of the presence of government. Cheap government and maximum personal liberty were the goals of Cartwright. Political reform was to be used to achieve these ends.

CHAPTER 4

A LOST OPPORTUNITY: CARTWRIGHT AND THE INDUSTRIAL REVOLUTION

During the last twenty years of the century, while Cartwright was becoming recognized as a Radical spokesman, a change was going on beneath the surface of society. This was the Industrial Revolution, whose consequences for Englishmen of all classes were deep and far-reaching. At the time, however, it appears that no one could grasp its meaning. The change from small-scale domestic manufacturing to the factory system had been developing for some time, and with the harnessing of steam power to production in the 1760s the stage was set for that rapid increase in goods which occurred after 1780. In cotton textiles alone, imports of raw cotton increased more than eightfold between 1780 and 1800 and nine-tenths of cotton production for the century resulted in these two decades.

Even the simple economic results of this change were not clear to a great many people and the extraordinarily wide range of social effects were almost unappreciated. Quietly, a major crisis in the life of the nation had been reached but few Englishmen were aware of what was occurring. At stake was much more than a change in the means of production with some obvious social consequences: it was nothing less than a reweaving of the entire fabric of society. The Industrial Revolution created new needs and resulted in a transformation of values affecting law, education, manners and morals – even the arts, sports and styles of dress. It also posed problems with which only the central government could deal.[1] This was, in fact, the genesis of the large, complex and expensive administration which most modern people take for granted.

[1] For a discussion of this subject, see John W. Osborne, *The Silent Revolution: The Industrial Revolution in England as a Source of Cultural Change* (New York, 1970).

Politics could not remain immune from change; in several important ways it was permanently altered. Eighteenth-century political life was locally based, leisurely and inefficient. Thanks largely to the Industrial Revolution the role of the central government in the life of the citizen grew larger, while parliament became more efficient, honest and public-spirited. Paradoxically, as *laissez-faire* economics gripped the minds of England's rulers, the pace of legislative activity was increased and these same men showed a willingness to use the government for public ends.[1] 'How small, of all that human hearts endure, / That part which laws or kings can cause or cure', noted Oliver Goldsmith. This was a characteristic eighteenth-century view which was challenged and overcome as the central government began to consider poverty and ignorance as evils which might be reduced rather than remain part of man's tragic lot.[2]

The crude relationship between political behaviour and economic position had been recognized before the sharp increase in the output of goods and the application of steam power to the productive processes. It was obvious to contemporaries, if not to some later historians, that men went into politics to secure personal advantages. Yet there was no immediate clamour by bankers, entrepreneurs and factory managers to be more adequately represented in the House of Commons. This somewhat heterogeneous group, which was growing in numbers and economic importance, was generally content to be represented by landed elements as long as what they construed as their interests were protected. With every passing year the agrarian dominance of parliament had less and less justification in economic terms, but protest on the part of those who were in a position to effect change was remarkably absent. A major reason for this situation was, of course, the war with France. Men of property were almost united by national pride and by fear of revolution in desiring to see this war through to a successful conclusion. This was to be

[1] See David Roberts, *Victorian Origins of the British Welfare State* (New Haven, 1960).

[2] Lord Liverpool, Prime Minister from 1812 to 1827, echoed Goldsmith's words when he said, 'by far the greater part of the miseries of which human nature complained were in all times and in all countries beyond the control of human legislation'. Keith Feiling, *The Second Tory Party, 1714–1832* (London, 1959), p. 288.

the dominant theme until 1815, and parliamentary reform, Catholic emancipation and changes in the legal system had to wait. Indeed, throughout these years of war there were no real issues which divided political life into parties; dispute was virtually non-partisan and the province of individuals who might happen to feel strongly about certain questions. It was not until about 1820 that politics showed a semblance of two-party activity. At this time, with the war emergency over, many businessmen began to feel that the dominant Tory party was not paying sufficient attention to their interests.[1]

Thus, while eventually the changes brought about by the Industrial Revolution were deep and lasting in political life, there was not a great deal of alteration on the surface. Activity in the House of Commons was different in 1810, when George III celebrated his golden jubilee, than it had been when he ascended the throne, but not as much as might be expected. And it must be acknowledged that the movement toward making parliament more honest and inexpensive to operate was not originally inspired by any obvious connection with the Industrial Revolution. It was a result of an ancient feeling of disgust held by a minority for the extravagance and corruption in political life – particularly if it could be shown that these conditions were connected to the Crown. Economy and restraint on the powers of government were rated more highly than efficiency on the scale of values of the reformers. The latter quality seldom made an appearance on political manifestos until Cartwright was an old man. The zeal for competence as a requisite for the public servant had to await the advent of that larger, more concerned government which was produced by industrial change and contradicted that faith in Anglo-Saxon political forms which had gripped Cartwright and Obadiah Hulme.

Like the French Revolution, the Industrial Revolution was a turning point for English radicalism at which it obstinately refused to turn. As long as radicalism stood for the minimum amount of government (which was too small to provide even for public safety) and looked backward for a solution to the coun-

[1] Donald Read, *Peterloo, The 'Massacre' and its Background* (Manchester, 1958), ch. 6.

try's problems, it was doomed to remain an impotent force. Industrial developments demanded a new response but the old politics captivated Tory and Radical alike. The groups of workers who articulated their grievances did so in old-fashioned political terms and with pre-industrial living conditions in mind. Perhaps not until the failure of Chartism in the 1840s did any substantial numbers of this class begin to accept the Industrial Revolution as a permanent reality which might have positive results. Even Thomas Paine, for all of his social welfare theories, had little understanding of economic affairs, much less the new relationship between the individual and the state which they had caused. He, too, was a child of the Enlightenment, hated paper money and approved of free trade, and longed for the removal of any government interference in men's affairs.

Such a tough social texture was the result of England's remarkable historical continuity. Elsewhere, other men grasped the nature of modern economic development and the changes in class structure that accompanied it. Although in these countries industrial change did not reach so high a pitch, social adjustment was rougher. But the sorely tried English industrial worker was content to protest and demand reforms which, couched in archaic language, are touching evidence of the modesty and forbearance of their sponsors. There is little evidence of a substantial, rancorous, class-conscious workers' movement during the early nineteenth century,[1] although there was much discontent over economic issues. That this discontent did not result in revolution owed less to government efficiency in rooting out subversion, than to the moderation of the hard pressed workers and their families.

Politics and economics met in 1799, when the government, thoroughly frightened by the possibility of the spread of Jacobinism across the English Channel, suppressed Corresponding Societies as well as combinations of working men. The action directed against the former continued policies which had begun earlier in the decade, while the suppression of workers' organiza-

[1] A different point of view is maintained by E. P. Thompson. See *The Making of the English Working Class* (London, 1963).

tions was a Draconian remedy for the growing problem of industrial unrest. Not content with existing legislation against possible unions of workers, the new laws forbade combinations which were designed to secure shorter hours or higher wages. The effect of the Combination Laws was to permit the masters to exercise summary jurisdiction over their own employees, for they provided that two magistrates could try workers accused of the offence of combining to restrain trade. Many masters doubled as unpaid magistrates. Thus, in contrast to the usual leisurely working of the legal system, industrial offences were to be dealt with expeditiously. The fact that these laws were in theory also designed to cover restraints of trade on the part of the factory owners deceived no one. Their operation was directed almost exclusively against the workers.

With the Whigs in disarray after the secession of the Foxites two years earlier, there was little opposition to this unfair legislation in parliament. Even opponents of the Combination Acts were so untouched by new ideas that they cited Adam Smith as justification for rejection of the bill. Nor did the radicals elsewhere object strenuously, much less seize the opportunity to make common cause with the growing numbers of industrial workers, by denouncing one more example of repression. Political radicalism was at a low ebb and its proponents bereft of the necessary imagination to extend its appeal. In addition, given the firm support for traditional values concerning property, it would not be remarkable if putative radicals should have agreed with Wilberforce that workers' combinations were a disease in society. Cartwright did not speak out on this issue. He was himself the prosperous proprietor of an estate and had already taken steps to limit the wages of his own employees.[1] At this stage of his career he ignored the working classes.

The opportunity for a new avenue of attack for radicalism having been overlooked, Cartwright's activities during the last few years of the century were confined to futile attempts to promote public meetings. In the mid-1790s he had been busy with personal matters; he was to be again after 1799, but during

[1] See p. 37.

the interlude Cartwright was hard at work trying to form societies and hold reform conventions. This may have done little to advance his cause, but Cartwright found the climate of the times hostile even to this activity. Shadows, not substance, dominated discussion. The details of various plans to organize protest meetings show little relation either to political reality or to the genuine grievances of the majority of people in the country.[1]

The man who would in the future oppose taxes on capital, denounce the Luddites, and disassociate himself from the land-sharing schemes of the Spenceans, was quick to take exception to anything which might be construed as 'an attempt to excite the poor to invade the property of the rich'. Even the phrase 'domineering rich' in a manifesto drew Cartwright's hostility.[2] Political reform was to Cartwright the all in all. In an 1801 letter to the radical shoemaker, Thomas Hardy, he summed up his feelings on the amount of reform which was desirable: 'I do not agree with many, who think it is even now too late so to compose the public mind as to be able to stop at *Reform*, instead of driving on to a *Revolution*; since I am thoroughly convinced, that a complete reform in the representative part of our government, would still save some certain privileged parties, how little soever they may be thought by some to deserve saving.'[3] The temptation to demagogy was resisted all through his career.

Some people might argue that a sentence in his *An Appeal Civil and Military on the Subject of the English Constitution* contradicts this judgment about demagogy. 'What is', he asserts, 'the end of all government, but the good and happiness of THE PEOPLE?' He follows this with, 'Are not the crowns of kings, and the coronets of nobles, set on their heads to promote *this* end?' It would be rash to accuse Cartwright of an appeal to the masses on the basis of statements like these scattered throughout his works. He always directed his writings toward well-placed persons or a group (in the case of *An Appeal* to officers in the British army), never toward the masses. His book was so poorly

[1] *L and C*, vol. 1, pp. 235ff. They do, however, reflect courage in defying the authority of the state and the terror of vigilante groups.

[2] *Ibid.* p. 245.

[3] *Ibid.* p. 292.

organized that these striking sentences and another ('the human heart, panting for freedom as the sparks fly upwards...') were placed almost at the end.[1] Remarkably democratic in his political views (he had few economic or social ones), Cartwright remained faithful to his class.

In the opening pages of this long book he affirms his preference for 'the wise and manly practise of our ancestors', and for 'the neglected law of the land'.[2] Perhaps reacting against Jacobinism, Cartwright's writings would more and more be inspired by the Anglo-Saxon past and veneration for 'the god-like Alfred'.[3] The political and military organization of pre-Conquest England had become the ideal to which he would return again and again. Since Englishmen had once elected their legislative, judicial and military commanders they must do so again.[4] But not all of England's past was glorious; certainly not the introduction of taxation and corruption which succeeded the expulsion of the Stuarts.[5] Here he once again reflects that mistrust of finance and commerce which was such an important part of radical reform. Again we see the comparison to the Tories Swift and Bolingbroke and to the populist reform movements which were to come. The suspicion of anything to do with trade may be seen as a factor which handicapped the response of Cartwright to the Industrial Revolution and suggests a reason for his absorption in strictly political solutions to problems.

He blamed England for the war with France and was still friendly in principle to the French Revolution. Yet foreign affairs, as usual, were not his main interest but were something to be dismissed by *obiter dicta*; his real concern was with reform at home. This was also demonstrated by his correspondence. Cartwright was on good terms with Fox and took pains to cultivate his acquaintance, sending Fox letters as well as copies of all his pamphlets and being rewarded with short replies from the genial politician who was now in a self-imposed exile from parliament. The two men agreed about the war and press freedom,

[1] *An Appeal*, etc. (2nd ed.) (London, 1799), pp. 289, 269.
[2] *Ibid.* p. 6.
[3] *Ibid.* p. 132.
[4] *Ibid.* pp. 219–26. Until the Forty Shilling Act of 1430 every free man could vote. p. 32.
[5] *Ibid.* p. 3.

although Fox, of course, did not accept universal male suffrage or some of the other measures which Cartwright deemed essential. He was also in correspondence with lesser figures such as the philanthropist Granville Sharp and Charles, Earl of Stanhope. The latter was an unconventional person redolent of the atmosphere of the eighteenth century: political reformer, inventor, and disinheritor of his children. Fox and Stanhope were from a different world than Cartwright. Cosmopolitan, they had lived and studied on the continent and their Francophilia was part of the internationalism of their class. Cartwright, on the other hand, had absorbed the crude prejudices of most Englishmen towards the ancient enemy and his contact with Frenchmen was dominated by his experiences at the battle of Quiberon Bay. His own sympathy for France was confined to the ideals of the French Revolution. This mood was related to his conviction that England's attention should be on reform rather than war with France.[1]

Yet *An Appeal* did have forward-looking elements. Perhaps the key passage in the book is 'It is certainly not because I have some acres of land, – or because I might have been born in one borough, – or have boiled a pot in another, – or been apprenticed to a blacksmith in a third, or in a fourth had married the daughter of a fisherman, – or on any such nonsensical pretension, I have a right to vote in the choice of representatives. No: It is because I am a MAN...'[2] Cartwright stated here in more decisive terms what had already been suggested in *Take Your Choice!* It was the principle that the right to vote should be based on the individual personality. Virtual representation or any other system of franchise which rested on a collective franchise for groups or interests was thereby denied. Noteworthy also was his insistence upon a written constitution, which could be understood by ordinary men and the belief in the separation of the legislative from the executive branch of government.[3] The latter point was probably borrowed from the practice of the United States of America rather than directly from the theories of Montesquieu.

[1] *Ibid.* p. 85. Cartwright also did not like Henry Dundas, Pitt's friend, on the ground that he was a Scot trained in *Roman* law. p. 142.

[2] *Ibid.* p. 18.

[3] *Ibid.* pp. 12, 17, 11.

The legalistic nature of Cartwright's observations as well as some of his specific proposals brings up the question of how much he may have owed in terms of inspiration to Jeremy Bentham. Although the two men were not directly in communication with each other until 1811 when they exchanged letters on the subject of prison reform,[1] Cartwright had ample opportunity to instruct himself in those of Bentham's writings which had made their appearance in print. This was especially true of *A Fragment on Government*, which had been published in 1776. Toward the end of *An Appeal* his sentence about the end of all government being the good and happiness of the people might suggest Bentham's influence. But as far back as *Take Your Choice!* Cartwright belonged to the natural rights school, which was completely distinct from utilitarianism. As Halévy points out, 'To the divine right of kings Cartwright opposed the divine right of individuals, not the utility of the greatest number.'[2] Cartwright's respect for 'the wise and manly practise of our ancestors' – to cite again his opening theme – was deep and permanent. True to his generous nature and tendency to accept allies from almost every quarter, he did not quarrel with or nag Bentham. He certainly did not follow the lead of other radical writers and save his sharpest arrows for those who were working toward the same goals. Yet it must be recognized that despite later involvement with Bentham and his followers in the cause of reform, Cartwright owed little if anything to the genial eccentric of Ford Abbey. Frequent references to his hero, 'divine immortal Alfred', his faith in Anglo-Saxon England, and the belief that liberty was divinely inspired[3] separated this work from inductive, practical and unsentimental Utilitarianism.

Along with his confident assertions about the entire range of English history, Cartwright was also developing the idea that military reform must go hand in hand with political. The latter was to emerge fully after the turn of the century but even here Cartwright gives attention to a scheme to divide the country

[1] Elie Halévy, *The Growth of Philosophic Radicalism* (Boston, 1960), pp. 259–60.

[2] *Ibid.* p. 139. See also pp. 2–4 in *Take Your Choice!*

[3] *An Appeal*, pp. 10, 19.

into military districts for protection against foreign invasion.[1] But the thrust of this book is political and was mainly in the direction of restoring what had been lost rather than subscribing to novel doctrines.

An early sentence in *An Appeal*: 'To think, to reason, and to will, on moral considerations, and with independency of mind, is to be a man' might have served as Cartwright's motto. Such independence, however, cost him friends and caused him to publish and sell the second edition of the book himself. Far from a revolutionary, Cartwright was also no narrow partisan of law and order, and blind obedience to the *status quo* was never his counsel. Laws which disenfranchised the Englishman and deprived him of his rightful heritage deserved to be repealed. The great lesson of the French Revolution was that reform was ignored until it was too late; England must not do the same.[2] Reform, not revolution, was what England needed, for her principles of government were sound; violent conduct was both immoral and unwise. These principles put Cartwright into the healthy mainstream of English radicalism – a movement which he helped to form and to guide during the next turbulent generation. *An Appeal* was written at a time of stress when passions ran high and violence beckoned temptingly. Firm in his adhesion to principle but moderate and reasonable in conduct, Cartwright was a civilizing force in the country.

By the year 1799, when *An Appeal* was going into a second edition at the author's expense, Major Cartwright was fully occupied with family affairs. These consisted almost entirely of trying to ensure that his brother, Edmund, would be fairly compensated for his invention of the power loom. By harnessing steam power to the process of weaving, Edmund Cartwright had produced one of the most important technological breakthroughs of the early Industrial Revolution and provided England with a means of increasing its lead over all other nations in the output of textiles.

Edmund was an intelligent, versatile man, a fellow of Magdalen

[1] *Ibid.* pp. 99ff.
[2] *Ibid.* p. 178.

College, Oxford, a keen classical scholar and poet and, while a country clergyman, he was able to keep abreast of developments in agriculture and medicine. When someone explained to him that improvements in the process of spinning were so rapid that the weaving part of textile production was languishing, Cartwright applied his original mind to the problem and solved it. His first clumsy device was patented in 1785, but he quickly improved it until five years later he was operating steam-powered looms in a small factory. But for all his genius, Edmund Cartwright was a bad businessman and soon went bankrupt.[1] This was in part due to the violent hostility of the workers, who burnt his mill to the ground. No doubt Major Cartwright's implacable antagonism to labour violence was due in part to the way in which his younger brother had been treated by hand-loom weavers who were fearful of low wages or technological unemployment. Later denunciations of the Luddites sprang from unpleasant family experience with machine-smashing and factory-burning.

By the end of the century many other men had pirated Edmund's invention and John's business sense was employed in the arduous chore of bringing these people to justice and securing damages. His frail physique was almost unequal to the task, which precluded other occupations. That these efforts proved partially successful was due to his perseverance, as well as the excellent legal advice which was secured from the obliging Lord Stanhope, whose many talents included the law. It was naturally impossible to monopolize an invention which could be so easily copied and improved upon, but in 1809 Edmund was awarded £10,000 by parliament on the grounds of the importance of the power loom to the nation. He thereupon bought a farm in Kent where he devoted his remaining years to experiments in agriculture, chemistry and mechanical processes.

Major Cartwright was sixty years old in 1800 and in such delicate health that he feared his death would cause his estate to be

[1] Paul Mantoux, *The Industrial Revolution in the Eighteenth Century* (revised edition) (London, 1961), describes the impact which Cartwright's machine had upon textile production – and also some of his financial difficulties. See pp. 238ff.

sold. For some years he had tried to persuade his nephew, Edmund, to groom himself for the future ownership of the farm. It was not until 1801 that young Edmund finally determined against such a career. Cartwright had long taken an interest in the youth, who was obviously a substitute for the son he never had. When Edmund was at Oxford, Cartwright sent him an engraving of the Bill of Rights to hang in his rooms. Despite his yearning for a successor, over the years Cartwright offered his nephew advice about other occupations, including a rather surprising recommendation of banking as a means of acquiring a considerable fortune in a reasonable amount of time. Sarcasm was not Cartwright's style. While he did share in the view frequently held by radicals that finance was sinful and its practitioners in no small measure responsible for the ills of the country, he meant this as helpful advice.[1] Also, for such a devoted disciple of Anglo-Saxon political and legal forms he was curiously opposed to antiquarian research, holding that it did not invigorate the mind but lead it 'back into the ages of ignorance and barbarism'.[2] One may, however, look in vain for startling revelations of a personal or political nature in these letters, and the kindly Major was both too charitable and too discreet to burden his young nephew with scandal or speculation.

The letters do contain observations on current affairs which the preoccupation with family business ensured would not receive more lengthy treatment. For example, he was caustic about the secession of Fox and Grey and their followers from parliament in 1797, believing that they should have remained active in defence of the constitution. The root of the problem was a selfish devotion to faction instead of the good of the country. Never enthusiastic about the Whig and Tory parties, he wanted a broad-based movement for reform.[3] Like so many others, Cartwright had fallen victim to Fox's friendly personality and he never fully grasped the undisciplined, inconsistent nature and lack of principles of the man. The ideal schemes of government which were discussed in his books and pamphlets seldom mentioned parties. So deep was the disgust with politics based on

[1] *L and C*, vol. 1, p. 269. [2] *Ibid.* p. 272. [3] *Ibid.* pp. 264, 278.

interest groups that, like the authors of the American Constitution, he described a legislature which was devoid of parties, even those loose federations of the eighteenth century. His annual parliaments were intended to be filled by public-spirited citizens whose devotion to the country's weal would be paramount.

Another topic which attracted his notice and was recorded in these letters was Ireland, where war with France had brought to a head the festering grievances of Catholic and Protestant alike. Although the Irish failed to maintain their brief unity against Great Britain, the Catholics attempted a revolt in 1798 with some French support. This was soon stamped out but the prospect of his nephew being sent to Ireland with the militia caused him concern. Cartwright was aware of the tangled and ambiguous nature of truth where Ireland was concerned and cautioned his nephew about haste in forming his own opinions.[1] He had noticed Irish affairs in *American Independence*, when he looked forward to a union with Great Britain in terms of equality.[2] In 1783 he wanted the Irish to have annual elections, equal and universal representation and the secret ballot. Failure of these proposals to be adopted made him reluctant to speak of Ireland afterwards.[3] By the late 1790s he had evidently become aware that England's neighbour had domestic problems which would not yield to a purely political solution.

The Major's advocacy of his brother's cause in the courts, which continued to consume much of his time and sap his energies until he was well into his sixties, was typical of his efforts on behalf of Edmund's family. The adoption of Frances Dorothy years earlier proved to be in no way a sacrifice, for this sincere and earnest young woman was devoted to him and had minor talent of her own as a poet and translator. Her innate abilities flowered under the protection of Major Cartwright and his wife. This couple possessed in full measure the stability which Edmund lacked, despite his versatile brilliance. Their love for the girl was to be quietly reciprocated in print and her biography would

1 *Ibid.* pp. 283–5.

2 *American Independence*, p. 24.

3 *A Collection of The Letters which have been addressed to the Volunteers of Ireland on The Subject of a Parliamentary Reform* (London, 1783); *L and C*, vol. 1, p. 153.

have been a better book had she been able to view the subject with a modicum of objectivity. The letters to the junior Edmund are full of genuine concern for the future of the young man; only occasionally does Cartwright's longing for a successor break through and render them poignant.

Perhaps it was just as well for him to be removed from political life during these years when no genius existed to move the British nation toward reform. Cartwright may have sensed the futility of any efforts in this direction and perhaps did not feel so keenly the sacrifice which his brother's problems caused him. When great affairs are interdicted, little ones supervene. For years he had considered the idea of the government's erecting a temple to celebrate naval games and to provide a suitable venue for triumphs after important victories. In *The Trident*, which was published anonymously in 1802, he proposed such a building in a Greco-Roman style. Cartwright loved to plan and no detail of this grandiose structure was too small to escape his attention. It was like his treatise on naval surveying on a much larger scale. His narrow but precise mind delighted in the elaboration of a basic plan: at heart he was a mechanical draughtsman. The 'classical' style in which the temple was to be built was of a monumental nature that was quite foreign to ancient Athens and an historian of taste may see in the designs an anticipation of mid-Victorian architecture – perhaps even the Albert Memorial. The monstrous lack of reticence about the work, with its statues of whales, balustrades, bas-reliefs, friezes, personifications of the winds, engravings of Alfred the Great, and six newly-invented orders of architecture, failed to win adoption from a government heavily engaged in war with France.[1]

His absorption in this scheme symbolized Cartwright's divorce from the real issues facing the country. To his wife, who had complained about the shortness of his letters, he wrote: 'I am generally up at five, sometimes sooner, and working till dark. In order to get through what is before me, I must work morning, noon and night, so, when I fail to write, suppose me intent on the additions, corrections and polishings of the Trident, or "The

[1] *The Trident* (London, 1802). See also *L and C*, vol. II, pp. 350–7.

National Policy of Naval Celebration".'[1] Yet the same year in which *The Trident* was published he was also busily engaged in collecting evidence against those who had pirated his brother's invention. The connection between the power loom and a rapidly changing England was never made. Cartwright, with his political interests and first-hand acquaintance with mechanical progress, had an ideal opportunity to observe not only the total impact of the latter upon the country, but especially the potential for change in the sphere of politics. No reformer of his eminence was better situated in this respect.

New ideas would have considered politics under the influence of the Industrial Revolution and ways and means of deriving support not only from the unrepresented masses but also from propertied groups which might have seen an advantage in popular government. This would be especially true of manufacturers and commercial men who were excluded from the unreformed House of Commons. Given the prevailing mood of fear in the country this task would not have been easy. But the war against France which had fostered reaction also bred resentment in those who profited from making goods and those who carried them abroad and sold them. Economic progress would have been even greater had there been complete freedom to trade with the continent and America. England was not only the foremost manufacturing nation but was evolving into the banker, broker and shipbuilder for the world. Peace abroad and tranquillity at home were ardently desired. Conservative politics dominated not merely because of the appeal of Tory men and measures but because of a combination of ineptness and lack of concern which left the political arena almost devoid of an effective opposition. Cartwright was soon to re-enter that arena himself. Now, however, in his early sixties, his influence was not as great as it had been fifteen years earlier. His effectiveness had waned with the cause of reform.

[1] *L and C*, vol. 1, p. 303.

CHAPTER 5

THE REFORM MOVEMENT IN LONDON

By 1800 the effects of war and repression and the realization that the country supported the government's policy had thoroughly discouraged many of those who cared about reform.[1] The course of Cartwright's life during the first decade of the century was determined by his generally futile attempts to struggle against the torpor which existed in politics. Old political friends and acquaintances registered their lack of faith in the possibility of change; new ones were also found wanting in enthusiasm. Fox continued to be discouraging and, when finally placed in office in 1806, he proved to be a broken reed. The nominal Whig leader, Grey, was little more than a figurehead. Persistently pessimistic about the possibility of changing the political scene, Grey was far more devoted to the tranquillity of Northumberland than the hurly-burly of Westminster and only with reluctance left his estate to assume political duties in the capital. With the Whig group in disarray, Cartwright continued to place faith in county meetings but made overtures as well to individuals such as Place and Cobbett who were outside parliament. He also more clearly recognized the importance of London as the focus of power and cultivated extra-parliamentary methods to bring reform. Gradually, he was diverted from politically irrelevant schemes such as *The Trident* and became more single-minded in his concentration upon reform.

The century opened for Cartwright with the Earl of Stanhope and Christopher Wyvill pouring cold water on his plans for county meetings and universal suffrage.[2] Wyvill's attitude was especially galling to Cartwright, who had aided the Yorkshireman on previous occasions. He could never count on reciprocity.

[1] On this subject see S. Maccoby, *English Radicalism, 1786–1832* (London, 1955), chs. 8–11. This book focuses attention primarily upon those radicals who had some power. Thompson, *English Working Class*, ch. v has much to say about the English sans-culottes.

[2] *L and C*, vol. 1, pp. 295–9.

In the abstract, Wyvill continued to praise Cartwright's efforts. As long as the latter's proposals were couched in safe generalities, Wyvill gave them support, but where action was called for he could never be relied upon. In 1808, when the sixty-eight-year-old Wyvill refused Cartwright's plea to take the chair at a meeting, Cartwright was stung to reply, 'What is so proper for age and infirmity as an arm-chair? And what is so likely to make a man twenty years younger, as seeing around him hundreds pursuing with a well-regulated ardour and enthusiasm, the most virtuous and most glorious of objects, to which the exertions of his own life have been directed with uniform steadiness, and the universal esteem of good men!'[1] It was a rare rebuke from the iron-willed Major whom neither age nor illness could subdue. Wyvill would not go beyond the political limits which he had set himself several decades earlier; he could never emulate Cartwright's later willingness to associate the common people with the reform movement in the form of Hampden Clubs.

The crux of the difference between the two men was revealed in *A Letter to John Cartwright, Esq.*, a seventy-three page pamphlet which was published in 1801. In calm, lucid terms Wyvill rejected Cartwright's advocacy of universal male suffrage, partly because he recognized that it would be unacceptable to existing interests, but also because the Yorkshireman feared that the principle would lead to democratic tyranny and all the horrors of the French Revolution. When a progressive and thoroughly decent person such as Wyvill took the line that radical reform would bring about Jacobinism, one can see how narrow the appeal of radicalism was in the country. Wyvill made no secret of his fear of the ignorant poor; he wanted instead a householder suffrage. Wyvill was also plainly irritated by the enthusiastic advocacy of the abstract by Cartwright, whom he accused of being over concerned with theory. In solid English empirical terms he wanted the ingredient of experience added in order to secure the greatest practicable reform.[2] Although Fox

[1] *Ibid.* p. 381.

[2] *A Letter to John Cartwright Esq.* (2nd ed.) (London, 1801), passim. Also see vol. 6, pp. 226–62 of Wyvill's *Political Papers* for the extensive correspondence along these lines between the two men in 1801.

was praised several times in the pamphlet, like so many other Englishmen Wyvill seems to have fallen somewhat under the influence of the author of *Reflections on the Revolution in France*. Soon all of Cartwright's spare time was spent in prosecuting Edmund's case through the courts. These proceedings, in which the new and very conscientious Lord Chancellor Eldon had taken an interest, had already cost Major Cartwright alone £14,000. No case which Eldon handled was ever dispatched rapidly, but in 1803 an award of £1,250 for damages was finally handed down. Cartwright was stunned by its inadequacy, but at least this drain on his time and resources was now ended and he could channel his energies more fully into reform.[1] The award of £10,000 from parliament to Edmund four years later was gratifying but of no use to the Major.

One more incident interfered with Cartwright's becoming at last a full-time agitator. Napoleon's projected invasion of England diverted his attention to national defence and caused him to write one of his longest pamphlets. *England's Aegis, or the Military Energies of the Constitution* was in two parts: the first was published in 1804 and the second two years later. Part one was dedicated to Fox and presented to the Prince of Wales and most of the cabinet. It was plainly motivated by a concern over the 'gigantic schemes of the ruler of France' and a desire to frustrate his plans for an invasion of England. Elaborating on his plan advanced a few years earlier in *An Appeal*, Cartwright said that the Anglo-Saxon militia should be the basis of defence: '*for national defence on English land*, we depend not in the smallest degree upon any other species of military force than that which is inseparably linked with civil freedom in the very texture of our CONSTITUTION; which by making every citizen a soldier, has placed our security infinitely above the trumpery of the modern parade...'[2] Officers should be popularly elected; however, in the case of the cavalry, which was to be composed of men of rank and fortune, the officers might be elected by taxpayers. The tone of the work was patriotic, but its many denunciations of

[1] *L and C*, vol. 1, pp. 301, 314.

[2] *England's Aegis*, etc. (3rd ed.) (London, 1806), pp. 4, 14.

political corruption could hardly have appealed to the cabinet ministers. From a military point of view, Cartwright's love of the Anglo-Saxon world deceived him into suggesting spears as suitable weapons for English infantry against the greatest master of artillery that the world had yet seen.[1] The suggestion was serious. Henry Hunt records that the first time he met Cartwright he was invited to his home where, after coffee, the Major put on a display of attacking and defensive positions using the pike as a weapon. The pike was of 'a very curious and ingenious construction, with a sort of double shaft to protect the hands of him who used it from the blows of a sabre'.[2] However, it was Fox, in a brief letter which acknowledged receipt of the *Aegis*, who suggested the obvious objection: that a scheme to put weapons in the hands of the people was impractical at the best of times, but in the current crisis over democracy it was impossible to realize.[3]

The second part of the *Aegis*, published in 1806 after the emergency was over, was dedicated to William Windham, Secretary for War and the Colonies. Windham was an old-fashioned Tory who had nothing in common with Cartwright: raconteur, friend of Dr Johnson, a defender of bull-baiting. He had opposed the Treaty of Amiens in 1802 and was a violent antagonist of the principles of the French Revolution. Despite Windham's desire for a strong army it is difficult to imagine a contemporary who would be less receptive to anything which Cartwright might suggest. Perhaps the battle of Trafalgar and the shift of Napoleon's attention from the English Channel to central Europe account for the difference between the two parts of the book. The first section was essentially a military scheme with political overtones; the second was primarily a denunciation of the state of current affairs. There was, Cartwright now said, a need to reform parliament before a system of defence could be hoped for.[4] At considerable risk to himself he claimed that 'Those, to whom the preservation of the state has been intrusted, have not done their duty: They have even been grossly unfaithful to their trust'.[5]

[1] *Ibid.* pp. 31, 48–9. [2] *Memoirs of Henry Hunt*, vol. II (London, 1821), p. 79.
[3] *L and C*, vol. I, p. 315. [4] *England's Aegis* (2nd part), p. 11.
[5] *Ibid.* pp. 15–16. He clearly meant the recently deceased Pitt who had become the focus of hatred for all those who were dissatisfied by current events.

Knowing fully the danger of these remarks to himself Cartwright justified them on the grounds that England was in danger. Prolix, repetitive and, above all, angry at the politicians for not having taken his advice, Cartwright excoriated the selfish interests which governed the country. Noble sentiments covered page after page of *England's Aegis* but the work was retrograde and failed to suggest anything new. It remains perhaps Cartwright's poorest and least relevant longer work.

In 1805, Cartwright let his Brothertoft estate and moved to Enfield, now a London borough but at that time somewhat removed from the city. The change of address was significant. It was symptomatic of Cartwright's ever-deepening involvement in the political affairs of the metropolis and of that complete absorption with radicalism which was to endure for the rest of his life. The move also represented a real sacrifice of a preferred environment for the cause of reform. He was to reside at Enfield only five years, after which he moved into London. The year before moving to Enfield he had founded the Middlesex Freeholders Club to support Sir Francis Burdett, a wealthy baronet, who was a candidate for the Westminster seat. Burdett was a Whig with some advanced political views which deceived many of his contemporaries as well as some modern historians into believing that he was a radical. Burdett opposed the war with France as well as political corruption and flogging in the army. He consistently advocated a taxpayer suffrage but refused to support the principle of a secret ballot. After Waterloo he gradually lost his interest in reform and ended his political career as Conservative M.P. for North Wiltshire. Anyone who took Burdett to be a radical at any time deceived himself. Within a few years Burdett and Cartwright fell out over the amount of reform which was necessary for the country.

The year 1805 was eventful in other ways: Cartwright persistently tried to interest a variety of individuals in the idea of county meetings, he wrote another long pamphlet, and he began an association with Cobbett. None of the noble and distinguished persons whom he tried to persuade to call a meeting of the county of Middlesex believed that the time was ripe. They could not accept the Major's view that a few hundred signatures on a petition would act 'as a thunder clap to the terrified apostate', much less the government. With religious fervour, Cartwright continued to preach the good example of a county meeting. 'But we must not...allow this degenerate idleness and insensibility to the public interests to destroy us. We must bring forward the doctrines of salvation. We must put a friendly force upon timidity and lukewarmness.'[1] Stanhope, Grey and Fox could not be persuaded that this was so. Early in 1806 came Wyvill's definite negative on grounds of prudence.[2] Apathy among the great, however, did not at this time persuade Major Cartwright to associate the masses with his plans.

His pamphlet of 1805 was entitled *The State of the Nation; in a Series of Letters to His Grace the Duke of Bedford*. The Duke had been one of those members of the Society of the Friends of the People who had resigned when Cartwright joined. He was not ready to take a more active interest in reform in 1805 and was no doubt surprised at the writer's effrontery. The profits of the pamphlet went to the Middlesex Freeholders Club. It restated in detail Cartwright's former denunciations of political corruption and arguments for reform. Reiteration of old discussions was a feature of the Major's writing during this middle period of his career. Never a sparkling stylist, his tone was unusually dull in the valley between fresh viewpoints expressed in the 1770s and early 1780s and a few surprising innovations during the last decade of his life.

At the time the pamphlet was written, however, the danger posed by France was in the minds of many, so Cartwright gave a great deal of attention to this subject. His main point was the unnecessary nature of the war against France. Pitt was to blame both for the war and for making a deal with the borough-mongers at the time he took office to allow no reform.[3] These charges, though extreme, were commonplace among men to whom Pitt did not appear as an austere patriot, much less as 'the pilot who weathered the storm'.[4] History has modified such

[1] *L and C*, vol. I, p. 324. [2] *Ibid.* pp. 337–8.

[3] *The State of the Nation*, etc., pp. 30, 38ff.

[4] George Canning's phrase. It roused Pitt's opponents to fury.

harsh judgments, especially the one relating to the war with France, but to many contemporaries Pitt was the most hated man in England. Cartwright was exceptional among the radicals in seeing the struggle against Napoleon (which began after the breaking of the Treaty of Amiens in 1803) as defensive.[1] Though he was wanting in common sense, at times, Cartwright was not deceived by Napoleon and was never embarrassed, as were some prominent Whigs, by the lust for conquest of the self-crowned Emperor of the French. This was the chief virtue of the pamphlet.

It was in October 1805 that he began his friendship with Cobbett, whose weekly *Political Register* had moved from an extreme Tory position to one of criticism of the government over its handling of the war. It was in fact in that very year that Cobbett announced the existence of a 'system', composed mostly of commercial men, who had subverted England's ancient constitution. Cobbett was on the threshold of a career of highly personal agitation and his and Major Cartwright's paths were to cross many times in the future. Cartwright's letter of praise over the stand which the *Political Register* had made against corruption did not appear in this journal, which was filled with foreign and domestic news and printed few letters. However, in the following years several contributions by Cartwright made their way into the columns of the *Political Register*. Cobbett, who had been very friendly with William Windham, was in the process of withdrawing his support and printed a long letter from Cartwright which was critical of the Minister of War and the Colonies' plan for raising troops.[2] Cartwright thus became an unwitting factor in an important turning point in Cobbett's life, for Windham, several years earlier, had been Cobbett's sponsor and had introduced the younger man to the society of the prime minister and other chief officials of government.

Cartwright also was reaching an important stage in his own life, although with his surprising energy he was still pursuing lost

[1] *Ibid.* p. 4. He thus shifted from the position taken in *An Appeal*. The reason was Napoleon's seizing control of the French nation.

[2] *Political Register* (17 May 1806), cols. 731–45. Cartwright wanted greater reliance upon a citizen militia and feared a large standing army, which would, in addition, cost a great deal of money.

personal causes. He had met William Wilberforce as far back as 1785, when he predicted the sudden demise of the future champion of the blacks. Like Cartwright, Wilberforce's wiry good health belied his sickly appearance and he lived through more than one death-bed. Despite differing political views, the kindness and personal warmth of each man triumphed and a friendly acquaintance resulted. In 1806 Cartwright was bold enough to ask Wilberforce to use his influence to persuade the British Institution to sponsor the temple of naval celebration which was described in *The Trident*.[1] Cartwright's view was that 'The fine arts are a family of much frailty; and unless we can give them a virtuous education and a right direction, they will be full as likely to produce moral and political evil as good. By wise legislation, they may, as I conceive, be made powerful instruments of moral and political improvement.'[2] This was timid and philistine and his application was unsuccessful. The failure was his last effort on behalf of this lost cause and he was now ready for the significant move of withdrawal from the Whig Club.

Cartwright's refusal to participate any longer in the affairs of this society was not surprising as he had by now given up hope of the Whigs, as a whole, sponsoring reform. For years he had registered growing disgust with political parties in his writings. With the death of Pitt in January 1806, the Ministry of All the Talents, a predominantly Whig government with Fox as Foreign Secretary, took office but there was little evidence of a change of tone in politics. The objection of Fox to his Westminster followers' proposal that parliamentary reform be mentioned in their congratulations on the change of government was symptomatic of the fact that the old ways were to be continued.[3] Francis Place and Cobbett registered their growing disillusionment with a ministry which permitted the continuance of corrupt political practices.[4] When Fox died in September an ideal opportunity to get a reformer into parliament seemed to present itself.

[1] The British Institution had been founded that year at the instigation of Benjamin West to sell and give awards to modern works of art as well as to exhibit old masters.

[2] *L and C*, vol. 1, pp. 339–40.

[3] Graham Wallas, *The Life of Francis Place* (4th ed.) (London, 1925), p. 41.

[4] *Ibid.* pp. 41–2; *Political Register* (9 August 1806), cols. 193–200.

Fox had sat for Westminster where the voting was on a Scot and Lot basis, which corresponded roughly to a ratepayer franchise. For years an arrangement had been followed under which the Whig and Tory parties divided the two seats and thus excluded independents. Fox's death removed any qualms which the reformers might have had about attacking the government in power and gave them a chance to nominate one of their own to fill the vacant seat. Cartwright had been associated with Westminster as far back as 1780, when he served on a subcommittee of the Westminster Committee at the request of Fox. Nothing was accomplished then, but much had happened in the intervening quarter of a century and it was with interest that he watched developments in which he as yet played no part.

At first all went badly for the cause of reform. Lord Percy, the young and inexperienced son of the Duke of Northumberland, was a man who could be depended upon not to disturb the *status quo*. He was nominated for the seat by politicians who feared an independent candidate, along with Richard Brinsley Sheridan, who agreed to withdraw from the contest at the crucial time and leave the way clear for Percy. The open bribery of the voters with free food and beer by the supporters of Percy distressed that fastidious democrat Francis Place, whose tailor's shop was only a few doors from Northumberland's palace where servants freely distributed largesse. Percy won easily and the radicals groaned. But a better chance soon developed. In November the rickety and misnamed Ministry of All the Talents called a general election. The radicals were by this time better prepared and had a candidate in the person of James Paull, a merchant who had made a fortune in India.[1]

Cobbett, Place and Sir Francis Burdett, the major figures among the reformers, all supported Paull. Burdett's money, Place's organizing ability and Cobbett's talents as a political journalist were used to advantage. But Paull was a strange candidate. In his mid 30s, with a disputatious and suspicious

[1] This account largely follows Wallas. Cobbett's *Political Register* and James Perry's *Morning Chronicle* are good primary sources, but a book on Westminster politics is badly needed.

personality he seems to have been motivated primarily by hatred of Marquis Wellesley, the Governor-General of India, with whom he had quarrelled. After failing to get Whig support in his attack upon Wellesley he joined the radicals. He was already partially disabled as the result of a duel in India and would soon be seriously wounded again when he called out his sponsor, Burdett. After Paull's death by suicide, Byron referred to him as 'the Werther of politics': a rather generous epitaph for a man who was less a romantic hero than mentally unbalanced. But in November 1806 all was still harmony among the radicals and reformers. An open letter from Cartwright to Burdett gave his support to the wealthy baronet in Middlesex and to Paull in Westminster.[1] Cartwright also served as chairman of several meetings on Paull's behalf. When the seventeen days' poll was over, it was found that Paull had fallen short of victory by only a few hundred votes. The value of organization was clearly demonstrated.

Cartwright had drawn closer to Westminster politics but his identification with the borough was never to be as close as that of Place or even Cobbett. In the same general election he was invited to stand for Boston and Cobbett allowed him to use the columns of the *Political Register* for three election addresses. The honest major had no expectation of capturing the seat but used the opportunity for political education of the public. The voters of Boston had been accustomed to receiving substantial bribes from the candidate of their choice. Cartwright would not perpetuate this practice and admonished them that 'A vote is not in the nature of a chattel, that we can legally or morally sell, or can give away, for any private gain or gratification whatever; but it is a sacred right held in trust, to be exercised only for the good of our country.'[2] The only result of his political labours was another bout of illness.

Despite repeated failures to get elected to the House of Commons, Cartwright was still neither discouraged nor bitter, though a decade later he was to feel his exclusion more keenly. Six

[1] *Political Register* (8 November 1806), cols. 718–19.

[2] *L and C*, vol. 1, p. 345.

months after his rejection at Boston he stood again for the same seat during another general election but won only fifty-nine votes. National defence was still very much on his mind, although the subject had receded in public interest. He continued to send copies of *England's Aegis* to the leading government officials and had several long letters on the subject printed in the *Political Register* during 1808. Although Cartwright was not in general an admirer of French ways, the success of their revolutionary troops in defeating the professional standing armies of the Continent served as an inspiration. As we shall presently see, he was unwilling to forego discussion of this topic and would introduce it when he was referring to other matters.

Reformers in general continued to frustrate Cartwright because of their refusal to propose innovations. This was true of Burdett, who together with the naval hero, Lord Cochrane, was elected to fill the Westminster seats in the 1807 general election. It was also the case with Samuel Whitbread, the wealthy brewer M.P., who had recently gained more attention for his castigations of corruption. When his brother-in-law, Grey, was elevated to the House of Lords in 1807, Whitbread was passed over as Whig leader in the lower house in favour of the uninspired George Ponsonby. Like Burdett, Whitbread was on the extreme left wing of his party, but he was still a Whig. He was also too vain to work well with others and ignored Cartwright's appeals in the cause of reform. Toward the Major himself, Whitbread displayed aloofness mixed with condescension.

It is likely that the failure of Whitbread and Burdett to adopt his plans for reform of the constitution and the army accounted for some of the considerable amount of attention which Cartwright gave to Spanish affairs. His niece records Cartwright's vexation with Burdett who, in 1808, refused to bring forward in parliament two bills on the framing of which the Major had spent six months' incessant labour.[1] Expediency Cartwright once defined as 'an excellent servant, but the worst of masters'.[2] He saw it as leading nowhere and wanted the reformers in parliament to embrace truly popular methods and issues. This they refused

[1] *Ibid.* p. 355.

[2] *Ibid.* p. 378.

to do and he turned his attention to events in Spain. There, a popular uprising began against the French conquerors in May 1808. The revolt was directed against the new ruler Joseph Bonaparte and his brother's army of occupation. It was fought, however, without help from the squalid Spanish royal family, which had renounced the throne. A thrill of hope stirred many Englishmen. While England was politically inert, Spain was vital.

Public opinion in England, so long suspicious of popular movements, was in favour of the rebels and the government saw an opportunity to strike at Napoleon on the Continent. Under the close scrutiny of the radicals, the Tory ministry took steps to aid the Spanish and England was gradually drawn into the Peninsular War. To defeat Napoleon the Foreign Secretary, George Canning, would even ally England with Spanish liberals, although some of his countrymen were suspicious of a plot to restore the Bourbons. Cartwright himself was completely on the side of the rebellion. He made many suggestions which were admirable in themselves but, like those of the 1930s, did not consider Spanish history or traditions. Scarcely had news of the initial outbreak reached him than he prepared a twenty-four point programme for the rebels. But from the initial suggestion that Spain become a commonwealth to a final admonition that the new government patronize art and literature, Cartwright seems to have been talking about England rather than Spain. For this reason the document is of interest.

Instead of a king, he proposed a regent to be elected for a term of five years. As the chief executive, the regent should have his own cabinet to administer the state but no voice in legislation. The legislature should consist of one elected and one hereditary house and be solely responsible for declaring war and raising taxes. Each district of the country must furnish a brigade of militia, which would include all males from fifteen to sixty-one and every district would return a member to the Cortes annually. This representative must have landed property and would be elected by taxpayers, who must also bear arms. Officers in the militia must also own property and would be elected for five years. A regular army was not to be permanently established but would depend for its existence on an annual vote of the legislature. Finally, free public education should be provided for all children whose parents could not afford to educate them.[1] This latter piece of advice represented one of Cartwright's rare digressions from a purely political programme. Undoubtedly, this was the form of government which he desired for England, but he could not bring himself to go this far in his writings.

In a series of long letters which were printed in the *Political Register* he dwelt upon these ideas, especially the value of a citizen militia over a standing army. 'The nation which hires a soldiery to fight for it, gives itself masters instead of engaging servants.'[2] Events in Spain demonstrated to Cartwright the validity of *England's Aegis*. He was premature in congratulating the Spanish for their ability to free their country alone; presently Wellington's professional army would have to do the job, at times aided but often hindered by the native irregular forces. Also, the French armies, whose spirit Cartwright admired, were not composed of citizen soldiers as he imagined but of unwilling conscripts. But Cartwright was completely captivated by the idea of a militia and devoted as many words to this issue as he did to the ideal structure of government. Hereafter, the two questions were always connected in his mind, and he never believed that one could be reformed without the other.

By this time he had temporarily waived his insistence upon universal male suffrage – the one incontestably original contribution which the Major had made to radicalism – in the interests of harmony. Burdett's refusal to budge on his own demand that only taxpayers be allowed to vote necessitated this unusual compromise of principle. The wealthy baronet was now the uncontested leader of the moderate radicals, although he could not win the allegiance of his fellow Whig, Whitbread. Cartwright's modification on this issue was, however, counterbalanced by a growing admiration for a presidential form of executive. This is how we should view his advice to the Spanish to adopt the principle of an elective regent. The obvious diffi-

[1] *Ibid.* pp. 358–75.

[2] *Political Register* (17 September 1808), col. 458.

culties which such a course would create for England were not considered in his twenty-four point programme for the rebels in Spain. Any hint of Machiavellian tactics would seem foreign to Cartwright, but it is possible that the suggestion for Spain was intended as a trial balloon to test the reaction at home. Shortly afterward he wrote a letter in which the identical advice was coupled with praise of the United States presidential system.[1] If a test of sentiment for royalty was intended, the results evidently persuaded Cartwright to reconsider. Cartwright's future references to the subject were unremarkable until in the final year of his life, when, in his last book to be published, he made his most severe attack on the role of kings as rulers of a state.

At this time when transportation was improving but still slow and long distance communication was difficult, when the electorate numbered only a few hundred thousand and when national issues were generally less important than local ones, politics outside parliament were intimate and personal. In the absence of party central offices and paid professional advisers, extra-parliamentary organizations responded to the social institutions of their age. Political dinners and clubs were thus very important means of organizing opinion. The club, wherein men of similar tastes could band together in fellowship and from bow windows in Pall Mall or St James Street survey an alien world of plebeians and women, was becoming formalized into what would be a feature of Victorian and Edwardian England. Already, Brooks and White's were political and social centres for Whigs and Tories respectively, and the few hundred members of each were linked to one another in an age when the individual personality was of considerable importance in political life. Even the wealthy participated in the political dinners of the time and those that were held in memory of Pitt or Fox were major occasions. However, it was the radicals, too few and too poor to build a club house, who favoured this method of expressing congeniality and support of certain principles. To these men a dinner followed by speeches and discussion was an important way of restoring a harmony of views.

[1] *Political Register* (29 October 1808), col. 700.

In the winter and early spring of 1809, Cartwright was busy trying to promote such a dinner. His efforts resulted in a meeting at the Crown and Anchor tavern which was attended by 1,200 persons. Several members of parliament were there and Sir Francis Burdett acted as chairman. But despite the large attendance the meeting was not an unqualified success. Naturally, the nominal Whig leader, Grey, was not present, but Samuel Whitbread also declined to put in an appearance. The power brokers in parliament were conspicuous by their absence. Those who did show up were divided over the amount of reform which was desirable, as well as over tactics. William Smith, a veteran reformer, bluntly told the gathering that only a small portion of the nation's population actively favoured reform and warned of many difficulties in the way. And J. C. Curwen, whose act to prevent the sale of seats in parliament had just been passed, later denounced 'the inflammatory proceedings of a drunken meeting in a tavern...'.[1] It was ominous that the dinner should thus provoke the man who had sponsored one of the very few successful pieces of legislation to reduce political corruption in that generation.

In their reports on the meeting the radical press stressed the large attendance and the passage of resolutions which deplored the state of representation with its attendant corruption and abuses. Cobbett accurately referred to the resolutions as 'a chain of undeniable and notorious truths'.[2] The lack of a specific programme for reform made agreement possible. The throng was in accord over what was wrong with the country but could not unite on methods and goals of reform. The first two resolutions noted that the people should have a just representation in parliament and that the duration of parliament's sessions was too long. But how many more men should be admitted to the voting lists and what was the proper length of a session? On these questions there was considerable disagreement, so the fissures were papered over with the call for 'a full and fair Representation of the People in the Commons House of Parliament'.[3] As long as agitation for

[1] Michael Roberts, *The Whig Party, 1807–1812* (London, 1965), pp. 247, 249.

[2] *Political Register* (6 May 1809), col. 688.

[3] *Ibid.* cols. 686–7.

reform was couched in banalities the rulers of England need not tremble.

That often captious critic Francis Place praised Cartwright's efforts in organizing the dinner.[1] For his part, the Major took an active role in promoting another dinner which was held at Hackney in August.[2] It was not until the last year of his life that he admitted such methods had proved futile. Of a sanguine temperament, he continued to address rather sententious letters to the radical press on the subject of reform. To his surprise, just before the end of the year he received news that he was promoted to the rank of master and commander in the navy as part of a general promotion on the occasion of the king's Jubilee. But on the whole the first decade of the century was one of continued futility, opening and closing with disappointments.

There were many reasons why Cartwright's cause failed to prosper. One of them was the division among the reformers about how much change was necessary. This was related to the blurring of distinctions between left-wing Whigs such as Burdett and Whitbread (who were themselves quarrelling) and some of the radicals, and this subject will be examined in the next chapter. On the other hand, the radicals did not entirely lack organizing ability or the means to present their message to the public. Press freedom was yet to be won, meetings could be deemed seditious by the whim of a couple of magistrates. Yet this period, unlike the 1790s, saw no white terror and by comparison with any important Continental country there was a wide latitude of legitimate expression.

The principal cause of Cartwright's disappointment was the public apathy toward reform. This was a general feeling and not merely the mood of 'respectable' opinion. Exceptions did exist and within a few years the number of recruits for this cause would increase somewhat. But before 1810, on this issue parliament was by no means unrepresentative of the country as a whole. Recent historians who discuss class relations without emphasizing the abnormal war-time conditions miss the most

[1] *L and C*, vol. 1, p. 392.

[2] *Ibid.* p. 393. For this, Wyvill sent him a note of congratulations.

vital ingredient in the situation. The times were out of joint, economic life was disrupted by the war as well as by internal changes and there was no chance for a smooth accommodation. From the standpoint of these historians, more energy should have been devoted to solving industrial problems but winning the war was the most compelling objective for contemporaries. Cartwright, who was becoming known both respectfully and satirically as 'The Father of Reform', was frustrated by this situation. His numerous writings, especially *England's Aegis*, seem almost wilfully out of touch with reality. Anglo-Saxon political and military models, even if they had been correctly interpreted by him, were irrelevant even to this tradition-soaked generation. This last salient fact he never grasped.

CHAPTER 6

FOUNDING THE HAMPDEN CLUBS

In addition to a public coolness concerning political reform in England, those who were interested in the subject had to overcome the handicap of their own divisions. The collection of interest groups which composed the Whig party were themselves in disagreement. Grey, who stood at about the centre of his party, was doubtful that the time was ripe for reform, but so was Curwen. Other Whigs, among whom Whitbread was outstanding, were in favour of changes in the direction of giving more influence to that portion of the middle class whose basis of influence was cash rather than land. Corruption as well as unfair representation were their targets, and these evils would be reduced when property was represented more rationally. Some also desired to raise the quality of electors to ensure a purer political life. However, even the boroughs which were controlled by one person were not necessarily bad, and many Whigs agreed with the Tories that these boroughs admitted men of talent who otherwise could not have found a seat. The elder Pitt, it was pointed out, sat for Old Sarum and his son for Appleby, while Burke was member for Wendover. In 1810 Brougham would make his initial appearance in the House of Commons as M.P. for Camelford. To these Whigs, representation and its reform were looked at in an eighteenth-century light.

These arguments distinguished the liberal Whigs from the radicals. Also, the radicals were *déclassé* and Whitbread, out of favour with the magnates within his party because of his background in trade, could not afford too close an identification with the radicals if his ambitions were to be realized. Burdett was already beyond the pale; a Whig by temperament, his identification with radicalism deprived him of a respectability which was not as important to him at this time as it was to be a few years later. Cartwright's attempts to unite Whitbread and Burdett in the cause of reform had no chance of success and, of course, would not have meant much anyway. Whig and radical were sundered and the overwhelming majority of the House of Commons was hostile to any major political change.

In January 1809 an obscure member of the House of Commons, G. L. Wardle, made a sensational disclosure about the Duke of York's mistress, Mary Anne Clarke. Mrs Clarke had influenced her lover in favour of certain army officers who had bribed her to assist them in securing promotion. A thorough investigation in the House of Commons resulted in a verdict that the Duke of York was not guilty of corruption himself, but since he had been indiscreet he was forced to resign his official appointments, including commander-in-chief of the army. This was one of several squalid scandals at the time which involved those in high life and offered the radicals an opportunity of attacking the entire political system. The left-wing Whigs, Whitbread and Burdett, were also critical, although Grey poured cold water over their attempts to connect the issue with political reform.

Cartwright's own response, a thirty-page pamphlet entitled *Reasons for Reformation*, was so frankly political that an uninformed reader would have no chance to learn of the confined nature of Wardle's revelations. Placemen and pensioners, the influence of the Crown, an unconstitutional war and an unconstitutional income tax are the subjects of this treatise, which scarcely mentioned the specific issue that was agitating parliament and the public.[1] Cartwright claimed that many members of the House of Commons were placed there by the government and denounced the servility of parliament, but the issue was not squarely joined. Just as *Reasons for Reformation* never acknowledged the specific and limited nature of the Duke of York's indiscretion, these broad attacks upon the state of politics failed to recognize the growing independence of individual members of the lower house. This had been developing gradually since the accession of George III and was indeed causing concern to the leading members of the government.[2] Even more evident is the

[1] *Reasons for Reformation* (London, 1809), passim. Wardle was praised for attacking 'corruption', p. 3.

[2] This was due in considerable measure to the growing honesty of government. Archibald S. Foord, 'The Waning of the Influence of the Crown', *The English Historical*

inability or unwillingness to become aware of the fact that, in general, government policy was popular inside and outside the walls of the legislature.

The division between Whigs and radicals and the failure of the Duke of York affair to ignite political dynamite was demonstrated in 1809, when Burdett advanced a plan for parliamentary reform. This scheme called for annual parliaments, equal electoral districts, a ratepayer franchise and voting to be confined to one day. The seconding speech praised property as the only legitimate basis of representation and explicitly denied the desirability of universal male suffrage. Only fifteen members of the House of Commons, none of them important, voted for the measure but just as significant was the number of those who bothered to show up to vote against it – seventy-four.[1] Clearly, political reform was such a dead issue that there was no need for opponents to muster their forces. Ideas were not lacking, and both Bentham and Francis Jeffrey of the *Edinburgh Review* made imaginative suggestions. Jeffrey actually wanted the reformers to link political reform to the misery caused by economic forces.[2] Results could not be obtained, however, in this climate of opinion.

This fact seemed to be partially contradicted in the following year when Thomas Brand proposed another plan of reform which actually received one hundred and fifteen votes in the House of Commons.[3] But in this case, Brand's moderate proposals – triennial parliaments, property qualifications for voting, compensation to owners of those rotten boroughs scheduled for elimination – were aided by circumstances not directly related to the bill itself. In April 1810 Burdett had been committed to the Tower (where he remained for two months) after he had publicly denied the power of the House of Commons to imprison a radical leader who had attacked the actions of its members. The incident had comic opera overtones, as when Burdett was found at home by the authorities (who had mobilized every soldier

Review, vol. LXII (1947), 484–509; Betty Kemp, *King and Commons, 1660–1832* (London, 1957), pp. 103–5.

1 Roberts, *Whig Party*, pp. 252–4.

2 *Ibid.* p. 257.

3 *Ibid.* p. 275.

within a hundred miles of London) peacefully instructing his children in the principles of Magna Carta. It was the high water mark of Burdett's identification with radicalism. Not only the radicals but many moderate Whigs were alarmed because the ancient privileges of parliament could be used by a reactionary administration to stifle any dissent. A Tory-dominated parliament could thus use parliamentary privilege as a tool of reaction. This view was shared by Burdett's rival, Whitbread. Petitions urging the release of the prisoner also contained suggestions for reform and the Burdett case was more than a *cause célèbre*; it could become a catalyst for reform.

One of the most important petitions, presented by Major Cartwright and introduced into the House by Whitbread, was rejected on the grounds that it was an expostulation rather than a petition. Other petitions were rejected on similar grounds, but some members found themselves in the unwelcome situation of supporting petitions, the language and proposals of which they did not agree with, in order to maintain the right of public petition and free expression. With the radicals clamouring for change in London and in the provinces, the moderates were caught between two extremes in a political situation that was becoming polarized. Some joined Grey and Grenville in disavowing radical change and standing firm on what really amounted to the *status quo*. Others, unhappy about repression and mindful of the havoc which the war was causing with trade and commerce, were ready to support Brand's proposal. The mildness of the motion coupled with the unusual circumstances of the time it was proposed, drew perhaps the largest numbers of affirmative votes that was possible for such a measure.

Cartwright himself was stung into action by the imprisonment of Burdett. He not only petitioned against the imprisonment but denounced it in the press and visited the prisoner in the Tower on frequent occasions. With Francis Place he made elaborate plans for a reception to be tendered Burdett when the hero of the hour was released in June. However, Burdett had had quite enough of notoriety and, ignoring the crowds and promised festivities, arranged to leave the Tower quietly by boat. Place and Cobbett (who was also anticipating a large reception) never forgave him this desertion. Place did not speak to Burdett for the next nine years and Cobbett used the incident when he publicly turned on Burdett in 1817. The mild-mannered Major Cartwright made no dramatic demonstration of his disappointment.

Useful as Brand's motion had been, Cartwright could not allow it to represent the movement for parliamentary reform. It was necessary for him to assert that real reform did not consist in half measures and this he did in *The Comparison in Which Mock Reform, Half Reform, and Constitutional Reform are Considered.* The theme of the work was THE CONSTITUTION: THE WHOLE CONSTITUTION: NOTHING BUT THE CONSTITUTION.[1] Timid politicians and lukewarm reform were the objects of his scorn. Although *The Comparison* was marred by Cartwright's by now inevitable references to the need for a citizen militia and by his usual prolixity, there were also flashes of insight. For example, he scored off the adherents of Lord Grenville, the aristocratic Whig leader who one day would become in practice what he already was in sympathy, a full-fledged Tory. He recognized the danger to liberty of commercial men becoming members for rotten boroughs and identified real grievances in the forms of the war, high taxation and repression in Ireland.[2] Most of Cartwright's efforts were spent in trying to persuade Brand and his followers to avoid the way of Grey and adhere to real as opposed to mock reform. The latter was inherent in Brand's countenancing of disenfranchising as a step to reform and in the tinkering of some Whigs with Economical Reform. *The Comparison* was an overture to the reform-minded Whigs to desert their party leaders and to make common cause with the radicals.[3] Political tactics as well as political principles demanded a clear separation between reform and anti-reform if the cause of the former was to succeed.

In *The Comparison* Cartwright noted that 'All systems founded in the laws of nature, the work of the Deity are simple; that is, ultimately resolvable into a few self-evident PRINCIPLES.'[4]

[1] *The Comparison*, etc. (London, 1810), p. 5.
[2] *Ibid.* pp. 6–16.
[3] *Ibid.* passim.
[4] *Ibid.* p. 30.

In similar form this statement about principles was restated several times in later portions of the work. They are consistent with his denunciation of Economical Reform as a half-way measure and support the familiar negative view of Cartwright as a self-righteous doctrinaire. In the same manner his suspicion of politicians and political parties,[1] stated here and in earlier works, fits his picture as an impractical theorist. Both of these judgments are correct as far as they go but do not contain the whole truth. Cartwright in action was more flexible than he was at his writing desk as the next few years were to show.

Despite these strong words Cartwright had not given up hope for a union of the radicals with at least some Whigs who held advanced political views. In 1810 there still appeared to be a chance for this, although Cobbett, along with Leigh Hunt, was caustic about Whiggery. The *Examiner* was probably the best of Hunt's many efforts at periodical journalism and it gave political reform first priority. It was typical of the cleavage among radicals that despite the similarity of views between Hunt and Cartwright (including even a veneration for King Alfred) there was no communication between them and Cartwright was not mentioned in Hunt's *Autobiography*.[2] Literary radicals such as Hunt and Hazlitt never had anything to do with the activities of Cartwright and his fellows, and the two groups pursued different courses. In spite of the discouragement of some, the ever-sanguine Cartwright tried to bring together those who stood for reform. His efforts failed because some of the Whigs whom he hoped to attract found that the prospects of power which opened in 1811 after George III suffered his last and permanent attack of madness were too enticing and lost their appetite for change. Until the Prince Regent decided to continue with his father's ministers, Whitbread could deceive himself that he had a chance of becoming a member of a new cabinet and thus must acquire political respectability.

In March 1811 Cartwright was instrumental in causing a meet-

[1] *Ibid.* pp. 5–6.

[2] Neither was Francis Place, Whitbread, Curwen or Brand. Hunt never spoke to Burdett and never even saw Cobbett. *The Autobiography of Leigh Hunt*, ed. by J. E. Morpurgo (London, 1949), p. 175.

ing between some liberal Whig members of the House of Commons (including Brand but not Whitbread) and a group of London radicals. These men claimed that parliament must be reformed for the sake of the liberty of the people and agreed to meet again in April to plan for a reform dinner. The next meeting was a fiasco. Brand, under heavy pressure from his Whig colleagues to cease this flirtation with the radicals, withdrew and took all but three of his followers.[1] Although the liberal Whigs proved to be lacking in zeal, Burdett and Cartwright persisted in preparing for the huge reform dinner which was scheduled for June. The dinner passed off quietly but it had ambiguous results. Perhaps the only substantial achievement was the large and fairly varied support. Many of the leading radicals subscribed or attended the meeting, along with the naval hero, Lord Cochrane; James Perry of the *Morning Chronicle*; Thomas Coke, the progressive agriculturist; Charles 'Squire' Western, a defender of rural interests in the House of Commons; Combe, the brewer; the veteran reformers, Capell Loftt and Christopher Wyvill; and William Roscoe, the Liverpool Maecenas.[2] It was due primarily to Cartwright's timely letter writing that the actual attendance at Freemasons' Hall was so encouraging. The speeches, however, testified to the deep divisions among those who desired reform.

As a result of this activity the Hampden Clubs were born, but before turning to that subject it might be useful to examine Cartwright's thinking. It is best revealed in a well organized and forceful letter to Wyvill, in which he urged his fellow septuagenarian to become a steward of the meeting at Freemasons' Hall. Recognizing the ambiguity of the Whig reformers, Cartwright summed up the state of politics from a radical position.

> A vast majority of the House of Commons is made up of a combination of factions great and small, and of adventurers who bought their way in at rotten boroughs. All these stand on interests completely hostile to the rights and liberties of the nation. From a conspicuous feature, this whole combination we style the BOROUGH FACTION, although made up of rival parties who

[1] Roberts, *Whig Party*, p. 287.

[2] Subscribers are listed in *L and C*, vol. II, pp. 372–5.

have competition and hostility among themselves; yet whenever serious reform of the system is attempted, the whole combine, as one man, to resist innovation on that system.

The situation could not have been stated more succinctly and the dilemma of radical minorities within a parliamentary system was noted when he recognized that 'Instead of striking off the head of a Brand or a Burdett, it simply outvoted them...'

Under these circumstances how could reform be effected? The solution was to mobilize public opinion behind reform and this could only be done by cooperation with those who were also concerned with ending boroughmonger despotism but did not want to proceed beyond moderate lengths. Moderate reform was thus no longer to be scorned but 'Let us cooperate; let us reason with each other; let us promote discussion: in short, let us harmoniously yield each to the other, as far as possible, without a desertion of principle.'[1] The man who had only a short time before denounced piecemeal reform now recognized that circumstances necessitated a broad alignment against the twin evils of selfishness and apathy.

While realizing the necessity of an opening to the political right, Cartwright was also abreast of his times in considering public opinion as a force in politics. Closely connected with increasing newspaper circulations, public opinion had already been an important factor in the legislation against the slave trade. Twenty years after Cartwright wrote this letter, the *Black Book* noted that 'Public opinion and not Parliament is omnipotent...'[2] Cartwright was clearly disposed to work within the framework of the political system and use England's traditional liberties as a weapon to make government more responsive to the people. However, he did not possess a modern programme of economic and social change for a reformed parliament to enact and he regarded political purification as the end of his efforts. This vagueness about a goal for society other than a cleaner political life marked Cartwright as a reformer of the eighteenth-century stamp.

The meeting at Freemasons' Hall led to the founding of two

[1] This letter is in *L and C*, vol. II, pp. 5–10.

[2] *The Extraordinary Black Book* (new edition) (London, 1832), p. xiii.

more reform organizations. The Society of the Friends of Parliamentary Reform was founded in 1811, but the word 'Society' being considered too vague, 'Union' was substituted in the following year. It stood for annual parliaments and the extension of the suffrage to all persons who paid direct taxes. The annual dues were only one guinea, but no government pensioner or officeholder could join. Burdett and Cartwright were very active in the Union, which had a Cockney flavour, being full of Londoners. One of them was Matthew Wood, better known as 'Alderman Wood', a future Lord Mayor of London and champion of the cause of Queen Caroline. Wood's interest in progressive causes marked him as a typical liberal who could be won over by an appeal such as the Union was able to make. Another member was Henry 'Orator' Hunt who had participated in the meeting at the Freemasons' Tavern. Hunt was not a Londoner but a Wiltshire squire, then almost forty years of age. Tall and burly, he resembled Cobbett in physical appearance and was often compared to the one-time Peter Porcupine. However, while sharing Cobbett's quality of vanity, Hunt lacked his humour and mental dexterity. Even in his best known role of speaker at radical meetings, Hunt was not a complete success, having a disjointed style and poor diction. His most important work lay in the future and he and Cartwright were to meet many times.

Cobbett himself supported the Union, although he was in Newgate Prison, to which he had been sentenced in 1810 for condemning the flogging of a couple of militia men over a trivial act of disobedience. Francis Place did not join. He was not on speaking terms with Cobbett and considered Cartwright to be a nice man but a crackpot. Place had an abundance of common sense and a grasp of political realities which was denied to the persevering Major or the more hot-blooded radicals, but he was to make his mark by working entirely within the system. As usual, Cartwright had high expectations for this new organization but they were to be unfulfilled.

Much more important were the Hampden Clubs, the original of which was started in London in April 1812. Here again, Cartwright played a major role, even though he was at first more enthusiastic about the Union. Although he was a founding member of the Hampden Club in London, he seceded 'not as a deserter but as a friend' when it appeared that his presence would discourage others from joining. After a year's absence he rejoined the Club and was its most active figure until it expired in 1819. Indeed, the Hampden Club, which soon established branches throughout the country, represented the very thing that Cartwright had worked toward for many years: a united reform party which embraced many political views. The Hampden Club movement goes a long way toward refuting the charge that Cartwright was inflexible and unwilling to compromise his principles. Certainly this organization was not as democratic as Cartwright would have liked. All members had to have an annual income of £300 from landed property and the annual dues were £2. Unlike the Union for Parliamentary Reform, the London Hampden Club was supported heavily by peers and members of the lower house and there was a national basis to its representation. Among the other founding members were stalwarts of moderate reform such as Burdett, James Perry, Alderman Wood and Robert Waithman, a future Lord Mayor of London. Lords Byron and Cochrane joined shortly afterward. Cartwright's name appears strange in this company.

The London Hampden Club's moderation was well expressed in a series of resolutions that were passed at its initial meeting at the Thatched House Tavern on 20 April 1812. References to Sir Edward Coke, William III and Lord Camden were intended to assure the timid that this organization was historically rooted in the English tradition of freedom. And the meeting resolved 'That it is the determination of this Club to confine their resolutions and exertions strictly to the procuring [of] a reform in the representation of the people'.[1] The most important elements of this reform were the same as those of the Union of Parliamentary Reform: annual parliaments and a taxpayer suffrage. The influence of the London Hampden Club in keeping some Whigs in touch with popular reform movement and paving the way for political change after 1830 has been exaggerated.[2] The Club was not that

[1] *L and C*, vol. II, p. 26.

[2] As in Roberts, *Whig Party*, pp. 293–4.

important in the history of the Whig party. Its real significance was in the growth of Hampden Clubs in the provinces and in the missionary work which Cartwright presently undertook to spread the gospel of reform. This tactic would soon incur the wrath of the government. Some reformers, notably Cobbett, had warned against stirring up the forces of repression by forming 'cabals' and stressed individual exertion and open meetings. The elitism of the Hampden Clubs and the incessant '*talking* about what they are to *talk* about next time' disturbed the most powerful publicist in England,[1] who no doubt wondered why such an orthodox Whig as James Perry, proprietor of the *Morning Chronicle*, would join a society that was devoted to real reform.

After the failure of Thomas Brand's second and very mild reform motion to muster more than eighty-eight votes in the House of Commons,[2] something original would have to be tried. Here, the Hampden Club would be useful but Cartwright's first response was to continue to urge parliamentary action. In *Six Letters to the Marquis of Tavistock on a Reform of the Commons House of Parliament*, etc., Cartwright tried to persuade this member of the Russell family, who had seconded Brand's motion, to sponsor a vigorous reform bill of his own. The pamphlet was dedicated to the Prince Regent – perhaps the most sublime of Cartwright's several inappropriate dedications. In seeming contradiction with his actions in joining the Union of Parliamentary Reform and the Hampden Club he declared that moderate reform was impossible. The history of attempts to gain limited changes in the nation's system of representation was recounted and the point of his argument was that only drastic reform would meet England's needs. Triennial parliaments were scorned; oligarchy and heavy taxation were denounced.[3] A parliament which had just rejected Brand's milk and water proposal would hardly listen respectfully to plans to put the boroughmongers out of business.

But despite the apparent inconsistency, Cartwright had not

[1] G. D. H. Cole, *The Life of William Cobbett* (London, 1925), p. 214.

[2] Roberts, *Whig Party*, p. 295.

[3] *Six Letters*, etc. (London, 1812), passim. The *Six Letters* evidently had Cobbett's approval, for they were reprinted in the *Political Register*.

abandoned hope of uniting all reformers and the *Six Letters* may be seen as the hasty gesture of an irritated man who had recently witnessed several defeats of political moderation. Writing to Wyvill he continued to uphold the moderate principles of the Union and the Hampden Club, though he condemned Brand's proposals as a 'palliative'.[1] He could not know that the year 1812 represented the last time that a reform bill would be advanced in parliament for years and that the presumed stalwarts, Brand and Whitbread, would be diverted into other causes. At the time, Cartwright was even out of sympathy with the Hampden Club because of its restrictions upon membership and refusal to be committed to radical reform. Ironically, the events of 1812 would make impossible any real reform and ensure his permanent identification in the mind of posterity with this exclusive organization.

During that eventful year when Napoleon's armies were meeting with disaster in Russia, and America and England were beginning their unnecessary war, Cartwright's attention, which was usually riveted on his reform programme, was diverted by social distress at home. Having in the preceding year travelled into the counties of Nottingham, Derby and Leicester, he noted the depressed condition of many workers there. Napoleon's Continental System and America's Non-Intercourse Act had served to close traditional markets to England's textiles. Handloom weavers, vexed by unemployment, low wages and the repeal by parliament of minimum wage legislation, took out their frustration on the property of their employers. A mill was attacked and two men were killed. To posterity the economic grievances of the workers are manifest but contemporaries saw evidence of sedition and noted with dismay the infiltration of criminal elements into what became known as the Luddite movement. The government, which made no inquiry into the economic causes of the protest, moved harshly to suppress it.[2]

[1] *L and C*, vol. II, pp. 30–2.

[2] Malcolm I. Thomis has provided a badly needed, book-length treatment in *The Luddites* (Newton Abbot, 1970). R. Church and S. D. Chapman conclude that the Luddites acted 'only to achieve limited industrial gains'. See their essay 'Gravener

To the humane Major Cartwright the rioters were like mischievous children wantonly destroying the property of others but, like children, they should be punished according to their ignorance and incapacity. The use of the army to subdue the Luddites was proof that a military despotism actually existed in England, for 'there is an *English* mode of preserving public tranquillity infinitely superior in efficacy to this *Continental* practice'.[1] In his eyes, taxation without representation was the real grievance of these starving men. After a fashion, this point of view agreed with that of an insensitive government which saw only a political plot. To the task of bringing back 'the deluded and the criminal into the path of duty', Cartwright lent his pen and was no doubt pleased when the authorities published his words and distributed them gratis over the areas most affected.

Given Cartwright's staunch defence of property on previous occasions, these sentiments cannot be considered as surprising as the tendency of modern historians to ignore or downgrade them. In August 1812 Cartwright moved a series of resolutions at a political meeting in Westminster.

Resolved – That the Chancellor of the Exchequer having taught us to expect, in addition to all the grievous taxes on income, an early tax on capital, it is expedient to distinguish between these modes of taxation.

That, to tax income, is to take a proportion of the rents or profits of an estate: to tax capital, is to take away part of the estate itself.

That a tax on capital, annually repeated, must shortly take away the whole of the estate.

That between the effect of taxing capital, and the effect of confiscation, this meeting is not able to distinguish.

That although the whole of men's estates may be taken away by arbitrary taxation, yet, as neither the land, nor its produce, nor other personal property, is thereby annihilated, so the real effect of the system is, to transfer all property, real and personal, from the right owners to those who, possessing a power of arbitrary taxation, can take away that property at their pleasure.

That the oligarchy, which, by usurping a great majority of the seats in the House of Commons, are become masters of all property, and can take it

Henson and the Making of the English Working Class' in E. L. Jones and G. E. Mingay (eds.) *Land, Labour and Population in the Industrial Revolution* (New York, 1967), pp. 131–61.

[1] *L and C*, vol. II, p. 18.

away at their pleasure, are, by the same means, become masters of the Crown and its Exchequer.

That, as the House of Commons exercises the authority of a court of judicature, with exclusive jurisdiction over whatever relates to the elective and legislative rights of the people, so as no redress of any injury, touching the same, can be elsewhere obtained; this meeting, on behalf of themselves and the nation at large, will present to that House a 'Petition of Rights', claiming representation co-extensive with direct taxation, in annual Parliaments, according to the constitution; and demanding that 'justice be neither denied nor delayed', according to Magna Charta.[1]

These resolutions demonstrate the gulf which separated the radicalism of the times from that of mid-century and later. They make clear the irrelevance of Cartwright and his followers to working-class needs.

Under these circumstances any proposal for political reform was doomed to failure. Yet the government, headed by Lord Liverpool after Perceval's assassination in May 1812, was not satisfied with stamping out 'sedition' but persisted in seeing treason in the most innocent actions. Although some recent investigators have given a macabre plausibility to the actions of the Tory ministers by asserting that there was a large, organized, militant, class-conscious workers' movement, at this time the available evidence does not support this conclusion. Panicky magistrates, *agents provocateurs* and tavern tosspots all contributed to the exaggerated concern among the fallible men who were simultaneously concerned with maintaining the *status quo* at home while winning the war against Napoleon. There was no surfeit of genius among the governors of England and except possibly in foreign policy the political arts were practised poorly. Certainly no one grasped the problems which had arisen as a result of the revolution in manufacturing techniques.

An instance of government over-reaction involved Cartwright in those political tours which were to make him famous. A group of thirty-seven political reformers in Manchester was accused of engaging in Luddite activities. Reform and not revolution was in the minds of most of the defendants but the authorities acted with severity. Cartwright travelled to Manchester to observe the

[1] *Ibid.* pp. 33–4.

trial. Half an hour after he arrived the good news that the defendants had been acquitted was received.[1] After a dinner celebrating the acquittal, Cartwright took advantage of his presence there to visit some of the Northern industrial towns. As a result of this experience he conceived the idea of further tours through these regions.

On 17 January 1813 he travelled north again and did not arrive home until 15 February. Once again he visited industrial towns in Lancashire, Yorkshire and the Midlands, stopping off on the way back at Bath, Bristol and Reading. Everywhere he courageously left petitions demanding a taxpayer franchise and annual parliaments in the hands of respectable business and professional men, and later claimed that 130,000 people had signed them. At Huddersfield he was accosted by an army officer supported by several constables who brought him before a magistrate. Since there was no evidence that Cartwright was engaging in any activity except distributing petitions the complaint was dismissed. The doughty Major was not intimidated and in letters to his family treated the incident lightly.[2] Lord Byron, however, simultaneously involved in love affairs and one of his spasmodic encounters with liberalism made much of Cartwright's case during a speech in the House of Lords. Amid his cliché-ridden remarks the future hero of Missolonghi exaggerated the severity of Cartwright's treatment at Huddersfield. The purpose of Byron's speech was to present a petition of the Major to parliament. This was directed against the impediments in the way of peaceful petitioning for reform and cited examples of obstruction by local authorities. The House of Lords tabled Cartwright's petition on the subject of petitions.

A feature of this trip was Cartwright's encounters with the working class. Here there was no meeting of minds. His niece praised the 'deference and respect' of the workers, but these people, who were becoming interested in political reform as a means of improving their working and living conditions, were not interested in the Major's own political goals. The latter

[1] *Ibid.* pp. 34–9.

[2] Cartwright's version of the Huddersfield incident appears in *L and C*, vol. II, pp. 47–52.

himself was at pains to point out to his peers that he was not slumming.[1] This homely but dignified elderly gentleman could never have the charismatic appeal of the big, earthy and gregarious 'Orator' Hunt, but even so it is disappointing that these initiatives were never properly followed up and that Cartwright remained ignorant of the masses.

Fresh support of reform was needed more than ever, although (as Cartwright may have recognized) a frank appeal to the working class would have done the cause more harm than good. Like Cartwright, most Whigs did not care about the industrial areas and their divisions on the subject of reform ensured that there would be no immediate sponsorship from that quarter. Only a small number of Whigs joined the Hampden Club; reform in fact was becoming an extra-parliamentary affair. Whitbread, when called upon to present Cartwright's petition in the House of Commons as Byron had done in the Lords, hesitated on the ground that such an action would have no good results.[2] Despite Cartwright's belief in 'self-evident' truths he was almost bereft of effective allies.

At this point in Cartwright's career two other salient facts emerge. The first was the inspiration afforded to nascent working-class reform groups by the Hampden Club; an inspiration which was due to Cartwright more than to all the rest of the members put together. Unsure of themselves, the workers were anxious to accept the leadership of their betters.[3] This attitude would grow during the next few years as reform developed in the industrial regions, a fact that was symptomatic of the growing independence of the provinces from London that was to continue until around mid-century. The other circumstance involved new evidence of Cartwright's willingness to work with and to accept the point of view of others. Again we see that he did not deserve his reputation as a self-righteous doctrinaire.

This flexibility, which was indicative of a new political maturity, may have been due to an awareness that effective allies were

[1] *L and C*, vol. II, pp. 45–7. [2] *Ibid.* p. 56.

[3] Donald Read, *The English Provinces c. 1760–1960. A Study in Influence* (New York, 1964), p. 67. In Thompson, *English Working Class*, the passages on Luddism stress the independence and initiative of the workers.

lacking. Certainly he was rebuffed time after time by those to whom he turned for support. The many printed petitions bearing the same message which were distributed wholesale among interested parties were more efficient than the traditional roll of parchment, but it was easier to get signatures on them than to have them presented to parliament. For the time being he compromised upon a taxpayer franchise and annual parliaments and agreed that further details of a legislative programme could come later.[1] This was a substantial change from his earlier meticulously developed plans for reform. But at seventy-three years of age Cartwright was not an exhausted old man ready for the compromises of senescence. The tempo of his life actually speeded up as he grew older. After disposing of his Lincolnshire estate and thus lightening his mundane burdens, Cartwright wrote to Mrs Cartwright in his usual engraved style. 'The storm is at length over, and the haven reached; if not the haven of luxury, it will, I trust be that of repose...To live to no end is a melancholy thing.'[2]

[1] *L and C*, vol. II, p. 70. [2] *Ibid.* p. 71.

CHAPTER 7

RADICAL PROTEST AND GOVERNMENT REACTION

A description of John Cartwright as 'cheerful, agreeable, and full of curious anecdote', about the time that the Major sold his house in Enfield and moved into London has been supplied by Francis Place. Responding to Place's invitation to dine by bringing some raisins upon which he munched during dinner and drinking weak gin and water, Cartwright was a friendly visitor. However, in political matters, Place found him

> exceedingly troublesome, and sometimes as exceedingly absurd. He had read but little or to little purpose, and knew nothing of general principles. He entertained a vague and absurd notion of the political arrangements of the Anglo-Saxons, and sincerely believed that these semi-barbarians were not only a polished people, but that their 'twofold polity', arms-bearing and representation, were universal and perfect.[1]

Francis Place was, of course, a political realist with little patience for idealism and at times looked at most of his fellow reformers much as Karl Marx regarded the utopian socialists.

Place's ruthless identification of Cartwright's shortcomings (the reference to ignorance of general principles was surely the unkindest cut of all!) cannot conceal his liking for the character and personality of the 'Old Gentleman'. Genial and well-disposed toward others, Cartwright was even more convivial in his own home. He was loyal and affectionate toward family and friends, and particularly in his later years loved a quiet conversation around the fireside or (at the other extreme) a romp on the floor with children, whom he allowed to mount and ride him while he was on all fours. This modest man did not describe the ideal life in books, as did his contemporary, William Cobbett. But in his dry way he had more genuine human feeling than the author of *Advice to Young Men*, who was perhaps driven by demons unsuspected by his readers. Cartwright was a practising humanist

[1] Wallas, *Francis Place*, p. 63.

who made many friends and few enemies; he had the inner tranquillity of those who are devoid of selfish ambition.

Rising before six regardless of season he lit his own fire. At eight a cup of coffee or chocolate was brought to him and at twelve he breakfasted. Except for an occasional walk he spent the remainder of the day writing or conversing. His niece later said,

> Of all men on earth he was the most accessible; no introduction or recommendation was necessary for those who wished to consult him either on public or private business, and though on some occasions this unguardedness was productive of inconvenience, it enabled him to be of essential service to many distressed and deserving individuals...no difference in opinion could even for a moment repel the impulse of his generous nature.[1]

This natural courtesy moved Cartwright to answer letters promptly and his simplicity of taste extended to a relaxing game of backgammon before retiring at night.

Since his naval service in Canada, Cartwright's health had not been robust. As he grew older he seemed to remain at about the same state of energy and strength. In his fifties he had felt worn out and complained of fatigue after a little exertion, but in his seventies, he was more active physically than at any time since his youth. His condition did not improve and he spoke of weariness at times but continued to drive himself. All who knew him were astonished at the prodigies of exertions performed by the aged Major Cartwright during the early years of the nineteenth century. He seemed perpetually en route to some provincial centre to spread the gospel of reform.

Spirits such as his were needed. Dismal as were the prospects for reform earlier, they grew even darker with the coming of peace. Even though England's mighty enemy was defeated, there was no relaxation at home. The concentration upon winning the war was no longer necessary, but the energies of the country were not spent upon remedying political and economic grievances. Quite the opposite, after Waterloo reaction was at its height: the fear of Jacobinism at home was in no way diminished. Adverse economic conditions leading to unemployment drove masses of people to despair and small numbers to pathetic revolts which

[1] *L and C*, vol. 1, p. 406.

were promptly stamped out by the government. Even the constitutional reformers felt repression in the form of the suspension of *habeas corpus* and the passage of new laws which were designed to curb dissent.

Under the surface, however, change was occurring. The alliance of country squires and Church of England clergymen with manufacturers and men of commerce, all of whom had been dedicated to winning the war, began to crack in 1814. The economic problems of the businessmen began to seem more pressing after the surrender of France, and they were not always dealt with by a parliament dominated by agrarian interests. Protection versus free trade, the importance of urban business in the life of the country, disputes between the established church and dissent, all became issues. This was mostly at the local level; parliament was still relatively unchanged in its philosophy. Still, within a few years these conflicts would make themselves felt in the protests over Peterloo and in the remarkable series of reforms carried through by the Tory administration of the 1820s.[1]

Cartwright could not be expected to be aware of what was happening or to know that the groundwork for the Great Reform Bill was being laid in the midst of the desolate political situation which he saw around him. Others more acute in their political penetration than he saw nothing but reaction extending far into the future. In parliament those who desired political reform were always in a minority. The Whigs, for whom this question was not a party one, but nevertheless had been advocated by enough of them to be associated with the party in the public mind, ran into a stone wall. Members of parliament who were by no means always committed to the government were overwhelmingly opposed to any scheme for reform of parliament or election procedures. On questions dealing with the economy or law reform, however, they might cheerfully vote against the government.[2]

Cartwright was determined to have the London Hampden Club act as the driving force and inspiration for reform elsewhere

[1] This alliance and its break-up is discussed in Read, *Peterloo, The 'Massacre' and its Background*, ch. 6.

[2] Austin Mitchell, *The Whigs in Opposition, 1815–1830* (Oxford, 1967), pp. 75–6.

in the country. To him this institution was not a grass roots movement of local newsvendors, unpaid secretaries and volunteer agitators. Rather, it was the heart and brain of the cause of reform which provided necessary leadership for the rank and file.[1] Cartwright had never been an egalitarian and shared Francis Place's view that the masses were too ignorant to be left to their own devices. While he would never have used Place's frank language to describe the common people's incapacity for political organization, the habit of authority was ingrained in the personality of the old Major.

His own desire to sit in the House of Commons revealed itself again in 1814. After Lord Cochrane had been expelled from his seat in parliament as a result of being implicated in a scandal on the stock exchange, Cartwright felt that he would make a good replacement. The loyal electors of Westminster, however, thought that Cochrane was the victim of a frame-up and again elected him to represent them. After 1818, when Cochrane resigned his seat to become an important figure in the South American wars of independence, it eventually went to John Cam Hobhouse who was a radical of quite a different stripe to Cartwright. The Major was willing to defer to Cochrane but a private memorandum written in 1814 is prophetic of what his feelings would be six years later. 'Very different would be my feelings...if, at the close of forty years' faithful service, and immediately after having stood in the gap against the treachery of an unprincipled intrigue, I were to be unceremoniously dropped and cast off as a worn-out garment to clear the way for some reformist whose patriotism, like some gay flower, expands only in the sunshine, and is shrivelled up at night, or in apprehension of a storm.'[2] Ambition for office was a permanent part of his personality, but it was never for self-glorification.

The incident involving Lord Cochrane was one of Cartwright's few digressions from strengthening the Hampden Club as a force for reform. He did take time from his political efforts to

[1] *L and C*, vol. II, p. 73.

[2] *Ibid.* p. 78. His niece's assertion that Cartwright would have been satisfied to work as a supporter of some qualified candidate is disingenuous. *L and C*, vol. I, p. 357.

design a country house for his nephew 'from the cellar to the roof' and one might argue that a series of letters written to Thomas Clarkson on the subject of slavery was another diversion. But this would be a mistaken opinion. Cartwright was impressed by the results which private efforts had brought in ending the traffic in slaves and was inclined to believe that the Hampden Clubs might work similar wonders with reference to political reform. He advocated making slave trading punishable at law as piracy, and a few years later the British government did just that. Yet Cartwright's *Letters to Clarkson on African and English Freedom* (1814) do not reveal as much desire to end the slave trade as zeal for reform in England.

The humane old man was sincerely opposed to slavery but much more concerned with the political abuses in England upon which the *Letters* actually focus. 'Subscribing to every word... which can be spoken in favour of NEGRO LIBERTY, I yet feel that ENGLISH LIBERTY has a still stronger claim to my exertions. In God's name, let us give to the *Negro* all we owe him; but to the *Englishman* let us not give less!'[1] It astonished Cartwright that men such as Clarkson and Wilberforce should be supporters of liberty for Negroes but not for Englishmen, whose condition he believed to have been worse than the blacks.[2] In keeping with his concentration upon political abuses Cartwright's point was that deprivation of full political rights was the most serious disadvantage from which Englishmen suffered. He did not, like Cobbett, who also chastised Wilberforce for his single-minded concern with Africans, focus upon unemployment, overwork, hunger and other abuses associated with a malfunctioning economic system.

Still, the Hampden Club remained Cartwright's almost sole concern and, indeed, with the decline of membership was becoming his exclusive property. In December 1814 only two others besides himself showed up for a meeting and in March 1815 Cartwright was the only person who attended another scheduled

[1] *Letters to Clarkson on African and English Freedom* (London, 1814), p. 27. Once again, Dorothy Cartwright's biography is not to be trusted.

[2] *Ibid.* p. iv.

meeting. This not only enabled him to carry on missionary work in the provinces unhindered, but to become the very personification of the club. Burdett, the national chairman, was evolving into an orthodox Whig, rather fastidious about whom he associated with. He would soon snub Samuel Bamford when the weaver-poetaster tried to discuss reform with him. In 1812 Burdett had still been sufficiently liberal to accept Cartwright's proposal of annual parliaments in return for the Major's acceptance of his own demand for a ratepayer rather than universal suffrage. Now, with Burdett's interest languishing, Cartwright was the centre of attention.

The decline of the London Hampden Club was not permanent and with the end of the war it revived and quickly became the somewhat reluctant parent of many local Hampden Clubs. These were primarily located in the industrial regions of the country and their members had little in common with the wealthy founders of the movement. The men who paid dues of a penny a week to the provincial Hampden Clubs were mostly artisans who were hard hit by the difficult economic conditions which followed the end of the war. Cobbett's *Political Register* was their Bible, Henry Hunt their orator and, for a brief period, Major Cartwright was their prophet. Their economic needs were forcefully expressed; the political means were copied from their social superiors.[1]

Cartwright was the only radical of consequence who was personally in touch with these groups, advising them on questions of procedure and policy. Cobbett, whose *Political Register* was printed in a special form to evade the stamp duty (nicknamed *Twopenny Trash*, its circulation quickly rose to many times that of any other journal), disliked the Hampden Club idea and urged his readers to put their faith in individual exertions and mass meetings. Ignoring discouraging advice, Cartwright pressed on with his efforts to get a wide base for political reform agitation but his programme was not what the people needed. By a curious irony, Cobbett, who had copied the idea of universal male

[1] Read, *The English Provinces*, p. 67. In E. P. Thompson, *English Working Class*, the sections dealing with the Hampden Clubs in the provinces stress their native vitality and freedom from the limitations of the London-based radical leaders.

suffrage from Cartwright's earlier writings, was now urging it in his *Twopenny Trash* while Cartwright, in deference to others, was still bound to a ratepayer franchise. The former was quickly raised by his writings to a position of preeminence among radical leaders. Although he seldom left London at this time, the great popular journalist became the man of the hour, while the seventy-six-year-old Major was trekking painfully from town to town.[1]

Part of the reason for Cobbett's eminence was his ability to discuss some of the economic grievances of the workers in language which they understood. In contrast, Cartwright's attention was riveted upon the Property Tax which fell mainly upon the middle class. The extraordinary amount of attention he gave to this item (today's income tax) reflected the conventional wisdom of the time which held that such an abominable measure could only be justified in unusual circumstances. Cartwright clearly felt that the war was no excuse for its enactment. Abolished in March 1816, the income tax was not reimposed until 1842. Since this tax is now symptomatic of the willingness of well-off groups in society to bear responsibility for those who are depressed economically, it can be stated with assurance that in 1815 the prevailing radical ideal was still small, cheap government. None of Cartwright's encounters with working men and women left him at all sensitive to their real needs.[2]

On 21 July 1815 Cartwright left for Scotland on yet another political tour. His aim was stated in a letter.

> Having myself, in the course of nearly forty years, had ample opportunities of observing among what orders in society the interests of reform can be pushed with the best prospects of final success, it is my conviction, founded on experience, that if we hope for good, we must, for a season at least, work for the most part by means of the middle classes. The higher then, in due time, will see the necessity, for their own reputation, of taking, in the matter of reform, their proper places.[3]

[1] Veitch's assertion that Cobbett borrowed Cartwright's methods and 'followed in his wake' is wrong. *The Genesis of Parliamentary Reform*, p. 347.

[2] Removal of the property tax was ardently desired by many Whigs. In March 1816 Cartwright took part in a meeting with (among others) Brougham, Lambton and Brand for removal of the property tax and abolition of the standing army in times of peace. *L and C*, vol. II, p. 122.

[3] *Ibid.* p. 110.

He visited Glasgow, and surrounding manufacturing towns, Edinburgh, and other locations on the east coast of Scotland as far north as Aberdeen. Everywhere he met with local reformers and left petitions to be signed. But there was no effective result and as the year closed Cartwright was again addressing himself to nobility and gentlemen and urging these people to bestir themselves in the cause of reform.

At this very time, farm labourers in the Eastern counties who had been discharged during the post-war agricultural depression began to destroy the property of their former employers. In the process of restoring order thirty-four of the rioters were convicted of capital offences and five of them were actually hanged. The agitation spread to industrial regions of the Midlands and North where unemployed workers demanded bread and broke machinery, looted and burned. Overseas markets had dried up with the return of peace, English agriculture which had expanded to feed the people during Napoleon's blockade was now over-extended, tens of thousands of former servicemen were looking for jobs – these were the causes of adverse economic conditions which followed a strenuous war and caused misery for large numbers of people. The government, as usual, saw only sedition and blamed radical agitation for stirring up a Jacobin-like discontent.

How justified was the government in taking this attitude? The traditional view among historians has been that the leaders of the Tory party – Liverpool, the Prime Minister; Home Secretary, Sidmouth; Eldon, the Lord Chancellor; and, of course, Castlereagh, who was not only Foreign Secretary but leader in the House of Commons as well – were men of limited understanding who were baffled by problems which were beyond their experience. Born and raised in more tranquil times, these noblemen were unprepared to deal with the consequences of either the French or Industrial Revolutions. Certainly they were all concerned with winning the war against France and preventing revolutionary ideas from growing in England. They were also to a considerable degree adherents of the *laissez-faire* ideology which took a negative view of government interference in economic matters, and in this age of emphasis upon property rights were more disposed to favour the employers than the employees in any labour dispute. The lack of police forces and local governments which could deal effectively with civil disturbances led them to place excessive reliance upon the biased reports of Justices of the Peace and to use the army to quell disorder. Thus, the argument runs, the authorities in London overreacted. Purely economic protests by starving men were regarded as evidence that revolution was imminent and, while genuine grievances went uninvestigated, repression was freely used.[1]

A different point of view has been advanced in recent years and has found some favour. This holds that the government was not as ignorant as earlier investigators believed. Where there is smoke there must be fire. Instead of blaming panicky magistrates and *agents provocateurs* for manufacturing evidence of a radical plot, one must investigate the working class itself. At a grass roots level we should find evidence of a well-organized, militant workers' movement of considerable extent and influence and with clear cut political goals. In that case the authorities were not as stupid as once believed and their actions become more comprehensible. In a curious way, socialist historians have provided justification for the Tory repression which liberal and conservative historians could not accept.[2]

This point of view is not devoid of merit and has a certain verisimilitude. Certainly, there are signs of widespread resentment among both agricultural and industrial workers over a large section of England. Unfortunately, evidence of a coordination of activities by these people is almost non-existent – much less a clear cut and articulate programme. Evidence of support for the handful of fire-breathing, physical force radicals who were based mainly in London is also scarce and one is led to conclude that the old-fashioned view is right: that mass protest against frequently inhuman conditions was couched in respectful, moderate language and that the response was crude repression. England's rulers at

[1] Some of these points may be found in chapter 7 of R. J. White's able *Waterloo to Peterloo* (London, 1957).

[2] E. P. Thompson, *English Working Class*, especially Part 3.

this time lacked genius and imaginative insight. Their general mental dullness excludes them from the bizarre justification of their actions provided by the socialists. These were not cool, alert men making rational calculations about dissent on the basis of massive evidence of a danger to established order. Instead they were extremely fallible politicians who were scared because they had witnessed a generation of revolutionary upheaval on the Continent. They tended to see the danger of repetition at home in any proposal for change, however innocuous.

The government was actually so bewildered by events that it considered Cartwright to be responsible for initiating and directing the workers' agitation. Force and violence were far from Cartwright's mind, however, and he had shown no desire to associate the working class in any meaningful way with reform. As we have seen, in 1815 and early 1816, while hungry men were rioting, Cartwright was still trying in good eighteenth-century style to remind the rich and well born of their duty toward liberty. Cobbett, too, at the height of his power with the people made it clear that he was bent upon restoring England's ancient constitution and abhorred any new ideas. Henry Hunt was mostly bluster. Meanwhile, the physical force fanatics of London were unknown to the people as a whole, and even today are so obscure that the loving treatment of them by some historians is reminiscent of biographies of exceptionally elusive saints of the early Christian Church.

As popular resentment moved toward its 1817 peak, Cartwright was preoccupied with public meetings, petitions to remove the property tax and comparisons between the current condition of England and that of ancient Greece and Rome. On 15 June 1816 the Hampden Club met with Sir Francis Burdett in the chair. Cartwright spoke in favour of annual parliaments and a ratepayer franchise, then introduced a Declaration in favour of these principles and against oligarchy and a standing army. John Gale Jones, a more thoroughgoing radical who had been imprisoned for sedition in 1798 and had spent time in jail for other political offences, was a speaker on behalf of the Declaration. In his report of the proceedings, Cartwright affirmed his long-held belief that taxation without representation was the cause of the country's sufferings.[1] Later, at dinner, he toasted 'The Constitution and the King'.[2]

Cobbett, however, was moving independently to take the lead among reformers by addressing the people directly. He had secretly come to the conclusion that Burdett was not to be relied upon to press for reform. With his many writings which reached a very wide audience, Cobbett had a clearly articulated plan for political reform. In the *Political Register* he flattered the working class by claiming that the labour of its people was the basis for a country's greatness. However, his plan was almost as narrowly political as was Cartwright's and his *A Letter to the Luddites*, which became famous because it urged the working class to avoid violence, demonstrated no real understanding of the problems of this group. Like Cartwright, Cobbett was a great force for moderation but lacked at all times a comprehension of large economic issues.

Two public meetings, which were held on 15 November and 2 December 1816 at Spa Fields, London, ended in riot. Although property damage was small, a person was killed as a result of the second riot. The Spenceans were clearly to blame and some members of this ultra-radical association were arrested for high treason, but none of them was convicted. Meanwhile, activity in the provincial Hampden Clubs continued. Home Secretary Lord Sidmouth collected evidence of sedition and anyone at all connected with reform activities was in danger. The moderate radicals were particularly vulnerable and became the object of slanders which associated them with republicans and land sharers. Many of these men looked forward to the new year with trepidation.

During the previous summer Cartwright had persuaded Sir Francis Burdett to start a massive petitioning drive throughout the country. In January 1817, the petitions were brought to London by delegates from the provinces. However, Cartwright's plan to invite prominent friends of reform to a great meeting

[1] *A Full Report of the Proceedings of the Meeting of the Hampden Club* (London, 1816), passim.

[2] *L and C*, vol. II, p. 125.

that was to coincide with the arrival of the petitions came to nought. Few of those who were asked to attend showed up. To make matters worse, Burdett refused to take the chair at the meeting, which was held on 23 January. The seventy provincial delegates, mostly working class, saw Major Cartwright, clad in a long brown surtout and a plain brown wig, march to the head seat with a benevolent smile playing upon his face. Despite Burdett's desertion, his proposal for household suffrage was introduced by Cobbett, who had reluctantly agreed to attend the meeting as an unofficial deputy from Westminster. Henry Hunt rejected this proposal as inadequate and made sarcastic references to Burdett. The absent baronet was spiritually very much present, for he had re-converted Cobbett away from universal male suffrage and sealed the lips of the benign Cartwright. The delegates, most of whom would have been excluded from voting under a household suffrage system, heard an obscure representative from Middleton named Samuel Bamford convince Cobbett that universal male suffrage was not impractical.[1] Resolutions in favour of this principle and annual parliaments were passed. But the victory of the provincial delegates and democracy proved to be illusory. Before adjourning, the meeting voted to communicate the resolutions to Burdett but in such a way that the latter could frame a new bill however he wished.[2] Meanwhile, Sir Francis, after spending three months at Brighton, whiled away the time hunting and enjoying the society of the Prince Regent.[3] Two years later in *An Address to the Electors of Westminster*, Cartwright was to admit publicly his error in continuing to place confidence in Burdett.

The meeting of the delegates having concluded in this ambiguous fashion, the way was clear for the presentation to parliament of those petitions which had been accumulated in London. Hunt bore the petition, which contained an alleged

1 Bamford has supplied us with the best description of this meeting. See volume two of his autobiography, *Passages in the Life of A Radical* (London, 1967 ed.), pp. 17–19. See also *Memoirs of Henry Hunt*, etc., vol. I (London, 1820), pp. ix–x, vol. III (London, 1822), pp. 417–21.

2 Elie Halévy, *The Liberal Awakening, 1815–1830* (New York, 1949), p. 21.

3 M. W. Patterson, *Sir Francis Burdett and His Times* (London, 1931), vol. II, p. 419

500,000 signatures, to Lord Cochrane, who was carried on the shoulders of the delegates to the door of Westminster Hall amid the cheers of the reformers. Cartwright's reaction to what was essentially the climax of his efforts is not known. Certainly it was an impressive occasion when Cochrane introduced one of the petitions and deliberately allowed it to unroll its massive bulk on the floor of the House to increase the dramatic effect. But the effort was doomed to failure. Printed petitions were uncongenial to parliament and the hundreds which Cartwright and his assistant, Thomas Cleary, distributed wholesale all too obviously originated in the same place. This fact was considered evidence of a conspiracy against the state. The petitions were rejected on the basis of having been printed and because of allegedly disrespectful wording.

Cartwright's work of the last few years was in tatters. To make matters worse, the government was attempting to suppress what little vitality still existed in the cause. On the day of the opening of parliament, while Hunt and Cochrane were receiving the plaudits of the people, a window of the Prince Regent's coach was broken by a missile as he re-entered the Palace grounds after returning from the ceremony. After sending loyal and congratulatory messages to the Prince Regent both Houses adjourned. Rumour was rife of a Jacobin plot and hysteria reigned among the well placed. In February, Lords and Commons both appointed committees to investigate evidence of sedition. Their reports were both swift and predictable: revolutionary plots and irreligion abounded, and in the following month a series of four coercive acts easily passed through parliament. *Habeas corpus* was suspended, existing laws against public meetings were strengthened, safeguards against treason which applied to the monarch were extended to the Prince Regent, and an eighteenth-century act designed to prevent soldiers and sailors from being seduced away from their allegiance to the Crown was renewed.

The radicals were again in disarray. Cartwright had journeyed to Brighton before the 23 January meeting trying to persuade Burdett to agree to universal male suffrage; the Baronet was adamant. Failing here, Cartwright had Cobbett appointed as a delegate (the other delegates had been elected) in order to support the limited franchise beliefs of Burdett. Both Cartwright and Cobbett believed that the Baronet's adherence to the cause of reform was absolutely essential to its success and were willing to compromise beliefs and tactics to pacify Burdett. Henry Hunt, who considered the Hampden Clubs to be a farce, held out for universal male suffrage with the same stubbornness which he was to show years later when he rejected the Great Reform Bill as inadequate. Following the 23 January meeting, many of the delegates, who came mainly from the North, accompanied Cleary to a meeting with 'Doctor' Watson and a handful of physical force radicals. It is not known whether Cartwright had any knowledge of this opening to the left in which his assistant played such a prominent part, but nothing happened except that the government used the meeting as an excuse to suspend the *habeas corpus* act.[1] The divisions among the reformers were deep. Of course, there was absolutely nothing in common between Burdett and Watson but even in the centre Cartwright, Cobbett and Hunt viewed each other with suspicion.

The government was using dynamite wholesale to kill a few crows, which could have been disposed of with a couple of well-aimed shots from an air rifle. Of course, the Hampden Clubs were smothered in the blanket wave of repressive legislation and Cartwright was once more in danger of arrest. It was to avoid a similar danger that Cobbett sailed for the United States at the end of March. He did not defect as has been alleged, since Cobbett never believed in the type of political activity which had helped to create the reactionary legislation. Still, his absence removed the most powerful newspaper voice from among the reformers, produced discouragement in the ranks and reduced their effectiveness. Although he continued to edit the *Political Register* from exile on Long Island, Cobbett never regained either his personal popularity or the large circulation of his paper after his return to England two and one half years later.

Taking Cobbett's place as the foremost publisher among the radicals was Thomas Wooler, editor of the newly founded *Black Dwarf*. Wooler was a less complex personality than Cobbett and

[1] Hunt, *Memoirs*, vol. III, pp. 412–13, 423–4.

his radicalism was simple and unalloyed without the desire to restore a mythical agrarian England that made Cobbett more reactionary than reformer. Although his appeal was primarily to the already convinced radicals and the heavy-handed style of the *Black Dwarf* compared unfavourably with the racy journalism that made the *Political Register* read by all classes and political persuasions, Wooler was very highly regarded by Cartwright.[1] The Major, who had probably had enough of sunshine radicals and self-seekers, saw in Wooler a man of high character who was willing to accept imprisonment in defence of his ideals. He permitted Wooler to borrow books from his library and subsidized the *Black Dwarf* by buying scores of those issues which contained a Cartwright essay. But Wooler was a poor substitute for Cobbett, and his programme would offend moderate reformers.

In the spring of 1817 the famous March of the Blanketeers occurred. A few hundred working-class men from the Midlands, carrying blankets to sleep in and bundles of provisions, set out for London to protest against economic conditions and political repression. The men were well acquainted with Cartwright's teachings and his motto of 'Hold fast by the laws' was adopted as their own. Their pathetic effort was quickly broken up by the authorities.[2] Shortly afterward the Pentrich Revolution, which also began in the Midlands, was crushed. The two episodes are accorded much attention by historians, not because they were in any way a threat to the government but due to their almost exclusively working-class character. The use of spies to smoke out the leaders was a feature of counter-insurgency techniques, as were the trials for treason which followed the smashing of these protests. Cartwright seemed unmoved by all of this, unable to identify with the workers' economic problems and, indeed, scarcely aware of their existence. His depression was due instead to the continued failure of political reform to gain headway.

[1] Wooler's origins were obscure, but he appears to have learned the printing trade thoroughly as an apprentice in London. Cartwright considered him to be an eloquent man 'of very superior attainments...' *L and C*, vol. II, p. 137. Dorothy Cartwright seems to have taken no notice of him apart from the times when he was associated in some enterprise with her uncle. She was clearly unhappy about some of the Major's later collaborators.

[2] See Bamford, *The Life of a Radical*, pp. 31–41 for a vivid account of this episode.

In July 1817 he gave vent to his frustrations in *A Bill of Rights and Liberties; or, An Act for a Constitutional Reform of Parliament.* Beginning with twenty-five 'self-evident' principles of government the pamphlet was an elaborately worked out plan for conducting popular elections quickly and efficiently. Although the specific political demands – universal male suffrage, annual elections and equal electoral districts – were borrowed from his earliest work which was written decades before, the pamphlet as a whole represented an answer to charges that mass participation in elections would cause the polling machinery to break down. Nothing which affected the electoral process was left out. There was even provision for a folkmote, which was to consist of all electors in each district meeting annually to nominate candidates for representative.[1] *A Bill of Rights* was a reaffirmation of Cartwright's deepest convictions. Six years later the Major had the satisfaction of learning that the work had been translated into Spanish, just before the cruel and treacherous Ferdinand VII was restored as king of Spain.[2]

A Bill of Rights and Liberties is a curious document to read precisely because of its banality. These were enormously exciting times in which to live, with the government suspending *habeas corpus* for the last time, arresting the disaffected and breaking up their meetings. Many persons who were by no means radical feared the consequences of these actions. Political repression on a scale unprecedented in recent English history took place against a background of economic suffering and massive industrial unrest. Food for the working class was scarce and expensive and the situation was aggravated by the 1815 Corn Law which kept out foreign grain in the interests of domestic farmers.[3] The quality of English life surely reached a low point during the first four or five years after the defeat of Napoleon.

Thus it is surprising to find Cartwright producing a pamphlet which lovingly elaborates a plan for political change, even to the

1 *A Bill of Rights and Liberties*, etc. (London, 1817), passim.

2 *L and C*, vol. II, p. 227.

3 See White, *Waterloo to Peterloo*, and E. P. Thompson, *English Working Class*, for accounts of these years which differ in interpretation but agree upon the impoverishment of many workers and the Draconian legislation of the government.

extent of showing an engraving of the polling table for the receipt of the secret ballot.[1] Nothing affecting the electoral process was left out of this scheme. Yet there is also a curious lack of relation of this plan to current conditions; it strikes the reader as being an academic exercise rather than a means to effect political change. The economic issues were, of course, beyond Cartwright's interest or understanding, but even on his chosen ground of politics he was inept. Never was the lack of topicality of his work shown to greater disadvantage than in *A Bill of Rights and Liberties*. A similar criticism might be directed against Bentham, but the great utilitarian never allowed himself to be involved in current agitation for reform to the extent that Cartwright did. In the case of the old Major, theory at times triumphed not only over practice but also over common sense.

Faith in the future is the opiate of the radicals and despite Cartwright's understandable distress he continued to hope for the best. By the summer of 1817, he had still not grasped the extent and permanence of Burdett's disaffection, but continued to believe in the Hampden Clubs when they were moribund and saw in the *Black Dwarf* an important ally. He also believed that parliament would be dissolved in the autumn because of a financial crisis.[2] At this time, however, the situation was improving from the government's point of view and there was no prospect of a new election. What was unknown to anyone at the time is clear to us now: the trough of the post-war depression was reached in 1816. By the summer of the following year iron and textiles were once more selling and the harvest was good. Working-class militancy died down in the autumn of 1817 and in January 1818 the government felt strong enough to repeal the suspension of *habeas corpus*. There is one other consideration to mention. By the end of 1817 Cartwright was once more his own man, for *A Bill of Rights and Liberties* reverted to his old policy of universal male suffrage and ignored Burdett's more limited version. For the rest of his life Cartwright was to pursue only his personal programme.

[1] Cartwright had a model of the table built in his home for the inspection of his friends. *L and C*, vol. II, p. 142.

[2] *L and C*, vol. II, pp. 137–41. A rare observation of economic conditions.

CHAPTER 8

THE PETERLOO MASSACRE AND CARTWRIGHT'S ARREST

Early in 1818 Cartwright addressed a letter to Sir Francis Burdett, who was to chair a meeting to protest against parliament's suppression of *habeas corpus* and the passage of repressive legislation. Cartwright had originally intended to be at the meeting but ill health prevented this. Despite his indisposition the letter which he sent in his place ran to eight pages and showed no signs of a desire to trim his programme to suit the prevailing government mood of reaction. Cartwright's new nominalism, which contrasted with his earlier organic views, was revealed in his assertion that national freedom is simply the sum of the liberties of individual men. Deeply rooted in the English past as was his view of liberty, it is surprising that he suddenly adopted such a characteristically liberal position. It is true that he had never talked about the Englishman's entailed inheritance and appeared to like the past because to him it signified liberty but there is a shift of emphasis.

The reason for this may be seen in the letter's main point which concerned an issue very much on his mind: the danger to individual liberty from acts of parliament. This body, being illegally constituted, had no authority to suspend the personal liberty of Englishmen. Of course, this is exactly what it had done by suspending *habeas corpus* and passing the repressive legislation of the preceding year, which caused the ending of reform agitation. For the rest of the letter Cartwright restated his belief in first principles and his faith in the efficacy of petitions.[1] He did not, however, lose sight of the new conditions which had been created by parliament's intensified reaction.

The *Black Dwarf*, which had criticized Cartwright early in

[1] *Major Cartwright's Letter to Sir Francis Burdett as Chairman of the Meeting at the Crown-and-Anchor Tavern, for the Relief of Suffering Under the Suspension Act, on Monday, February 2, 1818* (London, 1818). The *Letter* was printed in the 4 February 1818 edition of the *Black Dwarf*, cols. 72–7.

1817 for losing sight of his former insistence upon universal male suffrage, was now his principal ally. Wooler, who had ambitions of his own to sit in the House of Commons, backed Cartwright for the vacant seat in Westminster created by Lord Cochrane's resignation in the spring of 1818. He was a vigorous critic of government policy and had narrowly escaped imprisonment in the preceding year. Burdett also retained some of his interest in radical reform and presided over a meeting in Westminster in March 1818, when fourteen resolutions of Cartwright's attacking parliament for suspending the constitutional laws of the land were passed. On 23 May perhaps more than four hundred persons attended a meeting at the Crown and Anchor tavern in celebration of Burdett's eleventh anniversary as member of parliament for Westminster. Cartwright, Cochrane and Hunt were among those present and they heard the Baronet give a vigorous speech in favour of reform.[1] A sense of being oppressed is a temporary healer of personal differences, and there was a brief period of good-will among the reformers before the rivalry of those who were interested in sitting for the other Westminster seat divided them.

In his 10 June 1818 issue of the *Black Dwarf* Wooler, strongly supported Major Cartwright in the contest for Lord Cochrane's former seat. He admitted that the Major was too old for fox hunting, and 'He will not be able to finish two bottles of port after dinner, and then go down to the house [of Commons] and descant upon the luxurious allowance of two shillings and threepence a week to the poor!' But in terms of mental vigour, knowledge and zeal, Cartwright was the ideal person to represent Westminster.[2] Wooler was Cartwright's only ally of any importance. The Westminster Committee selected Sir Samuel Romilly, the humanitarian champion of law reform, to run with Sir Francis Burdett. Once again, Cartwright was passed over. Yet on polling day he swallowed his disappointment and voted for Burdett. When the poll closed it was found that Romilly had

[1] There is a description of this meeting in the *Black Dwarf* for 27 May 1818. See cols. 321–2.

[2] *Black Dwarf*, 10 June 1818, cols. 353–8.

secured 5,339 votes and Burdett, 5,238, and these two men were therefore declared elected.

Cartwright's earlier comparison of himself to 'a wornout garment' cast off to clear the way for 'younger and untried reformers' was understandable but not accurate in this instance. In the first place his health was precarious and the members of the Westminster Committee had reason to fear that he would lack the stamina to cope with the long and unnatural hours of a member of the House of Commons. This issue of health may have been a hypocritical excuse to exclude Cartwright but it is noteworthy that in August he was physically unable to attend a dinner in his honour, or even to do more than sign his name to a letter of apology for his non-attendance.[1] More important were the outstanding qualities of Sir Samuel Romilly himself. Here was no 'untried reformer' but a highly intelligent sixty-one-year-old veteran member of parliament with remarkable accomplishments to his credit. An advocate of Roman Catholic emancipation and a staunch opponent of slavery, Romilly has won lasting fame for his pioneering work in law and penal reform. His tragic suicide following the death of his wife the same year in which he was elected to parliament for Westminster deprived him of the opportunity of seeing at least some of his reforms being realized in the 1820s.[2]

Any person whose views were as narrowly concentrated as were Cartwright's would be blind to the accomplishments of the versatile Romilly. Yet even in Cartwright's own chosen field of political reform Romilly had won renown on the floor of parliament when he denounced the suspension of *habeas corpus* and other acts of government repression.[3] In fact, despite the unfavourable political atmosphere there was activity underneath the clouds of reaction. Henry Brougham's work as chairman of a select committee had resulted in a bill which formed a body of commissioners to supervise charities. Even the House of Lords

[1] *L and C*, vol. II, pp. 149–50.

[2] *Memoirs of the Life of Sir Samuel Romilly, written by himself*, etc., 3 vols. (London, 1840).

[3] Maccoby, *English Radicalism*, pp. 342–3. Romilly also made telling attacks upon slavery in the West Indies during this session.

could do no more than confine the work of this committee to educational establishments. Slowly the stage was being set for the progressive reforms of the next decade.

Although Burdett sang the praises of Cartwright at the August meeting, he had desired a friend, Douglas Kinnaird, as his colleague from Westminster. This choice was unacceptable to the Westminster Committee, the members of which proved that they were not merely personal followers of Burdett, by choosing Romilly as their candidate. Cartwright's support came largely from the voteless inhabitants of the borough. On 2 November 1818 Romilly committed suicide and a new election had to be held. Cartwright received the news while recuperating from his illness at the spa of Tunbridge Wells. He was naturally interested in this new opportunity but Francis Place had matters too well organized. Within two hours of Romilly's death Place drew up a bill which called upon the electors to support Kinnaird. Thousands of copies were printed and distributed the next day. When Kinnaird refused to stand, Place was not dismayed and quickly persuaded the Westminster Committee to support John Cam Hobhouse instead. These proceedings were a bit undemocratic for the borough of Westminster, which was supposed to be an example for the rest of the country. Over the opposition of Place a public meeting was held on 17 November. At this meeting Henry Hunt nominated Cobbett, who was absent in America, but Hobhouse was the popular choice. Cartwright, who refused to campaign for the nomination, was nowhere in sight. He seems to have felt that the honour of representing Westminster should have gone to him by reason of his long service in the cause of reform.[1]

The actual election was not held until 13 February – 3 March 1819. Thus, there was ample time for acrimony to develop and personal jealousies to make themselves felt. Burdett had been upset when Romilly placed at the head of the poll in 1818 and temporarily reversed his swing to the right. He was an enthu-

[1] See Wallas, *Francis Place*, pp. 132–3 and Hunt, *Memoirs*, vol. III, pp. 551ff. for a description of what happened at Westminster. Hunt's account is copious but untrustworthy; he was a violent opponent of Place and the Westminster 'Rump'.

siastic supporter of Hobhouse. Place wrote a history of Westminster reform from 1807 onwards which was full of caustic allusions to the 'corrupt and profligate' Whig faction. This provoked an official Whig candidate in the person of the Hon. George Lamb, the brother of Lord Melbourne. Henry Hunt, whose real motivations were unclear, spoke for the absent Major Cartwright. After the volunteer work of Byron's beloved Lady Caroline Lamb, breakfasts at which dozens of bottles of wine were consumed and disputes over precisely which persons were eligible to vote, the election was finally held. Lamb, who collected both Whig and Tory votes, was at the head of the poll with a figure of 4,465. Hobhouse received 3,861 votes and Cartwright 38. Since Lamb and Hobhouse held virtually the same Whiggish views the verdict was a defeat for Francis Place and the Westminster Committee rather than for reform.

While all of this was happening Cartwright was at the bedside of his dying elder brother, George, the explorer of Labrador. He did not campaign for the Westminster seat, which of course he had no chance of winning. After the election was over he was gratified to receive flattering addresses from groups of men in towns in the Midlands and North, where he had become popular as a result of his Hampden Club tours. These messages lauded Cartwright's services to reform and condemned the electors of Westminster for passing him over. Somewhat embittered, Cartwright uncharacteristically took offence at a few harmless remarks by Hobhouse, but the two were quickly reconciled when the younger man explained that he did not intend to wound the old Major. When Hobhouse was later sent to Newgate for a breach of the privilege of the House of Commons, Cartwright visited him there 'not to condole with him but to congratulate him' for suffering imprisonment on behalf of his political ideals.[1] In 1831 Hobhouse proposed an act to limit the hours of labour for children in textile factories. He had a long and useful career as a spokesman for worthy causes and one must conclude that he represented Westminster better than Cartwright could have done.

As his supporter, Henry Hunt, makes clear in his *Memoirs*

[1] *L and C*, vol. II, p. 162.

Cartwright had never had a chance of being elected to parliament from Westminster. The Westminster Committee (or 'Rump' as Cobbett and Hunt referred to it) had matters too well under control for a radical of Cartwright's views to be elected. Actually, as this election proved, Westminster was radical only by comparison with the rest of the political system. The tradesmen who comprised most of its electorate wanted a person of good, sound progressive opinions who might do something about high taxes and government extravagance. Despite his economic orthodoxy, Cartwright's political views were considered too extreme. Failure at Westminster was symptomatic of Cartwright's inability to win the support of the middle class.

Burdett was disappointed by the result of the Westminster election. He recognized that his great wealth was not sufficient to secure what he wanted in politics and that by moving to the political right he had won the enmity of Cartwright, Hunt and Cobbett. From America the latter rained abuse on Burdett during the latter part of 1818, warning Cartwright that his continued silence on the baronet's betrayal of reform would cause his own rejection by reformers.[1] Cartwright, who wanted to sit for Westminster on his own terms, was persuaded that he must dissociate himself from Burdett. This he did in a remarkable *Address to the Electors of Westminster* which was published on 4 February 1819, nine days before the election began. It was a document which should never have been published. Superficially an attack upon moderate reform, the *Address* revealed Cartwright's painful limitations and is evidence of his inability to grasp political reality consistently. While claiming that his friendship with Burdett had been political and not personal, Cartwright also complained of his unkindness. While deprecating Cobbett's vitriolic criticisms on flimsy grounds of style, Cartwright accused Burdett of personally killing his chances to become M.P. for Westminster after the death of Romilly.[2] Naive, self-righteous and almost simpleminded in his understanding of

[1] Patterson, *Burdett*, vol. II, pp. 473–4. Also, see the *Political Register* during 1818 and 1819.

[2] *Address to the Electors of Westminster* (London, 1819), passim.

politics and the psychology of others, Cartwright showed his lack of qualifications for public office. Neither of his fellow radicals, Hunt and Cobbett, made much impression when they were finally elected to parliament. But while there was more base metal in the character of each of these men, there was also an awareness which was denied to Cartwright. It is not surprising that his niece does not refer to the *Address* in her biography. For his part, Burdett ignored these attacks[1] and tried to recoup his position by moving unsuccessfully on 1 July that in its next session parliament should consider its own reform. However, the focus of interest in political reform had moved away from parliament.

Soon after the death of the Hampden Clubs in 1817, new societies were formed in the provinces. Called either Union Societies or Political Protestants they were well organized and included political education as well as reform propaganda in their activities. Unlike the Hampden Clubs, which modelled themselves on what the members considered to be the example of the original club in London, these new organizations were of local inspiration and demonstrated the vitality of the provinces. Their programme, however, was similar to Cartwright's long-held objectives and some of these societies claimed to have received his approval for their regulations. From the fall of 1818, these predominantly working class groups, essentially democratic in organization, gave self-respect to their members. Although accurate figures concerning membership of each club are impossible to establish, at a meeting of delegates from Union Societies held at Oldham in June 1819 representatives of twenty-eight Lancashire and Yorkshire societies attended.[2] Cartwright advised these groups to choose what he called 'legislative attorneys', rather than follow their original plan of electing their own members of the House of Commons who would attempt to seat themselves in that body. Cartwright's suggestion not only reduced the possibility of having charges of sedition levied by the government but the

[1] One of Burdett's admirable qualities was his capacity to forgive after having suffered great provocation.

[2] Read, *The English Provinces*, pp. 72–3 and *Peterloo*, pp. 47–8.

'legislative attorneys' would begin a new mode of petitioning 'in the form of a living man, instead of one on parchment or paper'.[1]

In their optimism the Union Societies expected that the monster meetings which they organized would force the government to grant reform. Open air assemblies were held in 1819 at various places throughout the Midlands and North and Cartwright himself attended one in Birmingham and accepted the thanks of the crowd. After his return to London Cartwright received word that he was about to be indicted for his activity at this meeting. Leaving his home at four in the morning he arrived at Leamington, ninety miles away, the same day. The indictment (in which Wooler and three others were also included) charged the defendants 'with being malicious, seditious, evil-minded persons, and with unlawfully and maliciously intending and designing to raise disaffection and discontent in the minds of his Majesty's subjects, and intending to move them to hatred and contempt of the government and constitution as by law established'.[2] At long last the law had caught Cartwright in its broad net. On 12 August Cartwright posted bail and two days later returned with his family to London. These circumstances would have prevented his appearance at the Peterloo meeting on 16 August at which he had been advertised as scheduled to attend. Cartwright, however, had declined as early as 17 July to appear at Peterloo and his absence at that momentous event owed nothing to this indictment.[3]

Since the government did not decide to proceed with Cartwright's trial immediately, he was able to give full attention to the events which occurred at Peterloo. Economic distress in the textile trade gave great popular support to radical protest activities. On 16 August some 60,000 persons gathered to hear Henry Hunt speak at St Peter's Field on the outskirts of Manchester under the auspices of the local Union Society. The size and almost military discipline of the unarmed multitude alarmed the local magistrates, who ordered the yeomanry cavalry to push through the people and arrest Hunt. The yeomanry cavalry was a militia

[1] *L and C*, vol. II, pp. 164–5.
[2] *Ibid.* pp. 168–9.
[3] *Ibid.* p. 166.

composed mostly of citizens in the region who owned property or were dependent upon those who did. Their anti-reform prejudices had been inflamed by the spectacle and in their haste to arrest Hunt they rode their horses into the crowd, striking out with swords at those who protested. Within a few minutes eleven persons were dead and over four hundred injured. Four years after Waterloo there was Peterloo, and a legend similar to the Commune and Potemkin had been created in English working-class history.

Hysteria and overreaction on the part of the magistrates and yeomanry cavalry were excused by an embarrassed government, which felt that it must show solidarity with the provincial leaders. Others were not convinced of the necessity for breaking up the meeting. Truth was served by a journalistic coup of *The Times*, whose reporter was on the platform near Hunt. The 19 August issue of *The Times* devoted most of its news columns to a description of the event and in an editorial the paper noted 'the dreadful fact, that nearly a hundred of the King's unarmed subjects have been sabred by a body of cavalry in the streets of a town of which most of them were inhabitants, and in the presence of those magistrates whose sworn duty it is to protect and preserve the life of the meanest Englishman'.[1] Some Whig politicians in parliament asked pointed questions. The radicals were, of course, united in denouncing the Manchester 'massacre'. Cartwright shared in the concern and, despite his indictment, participated in protest meetings which were held in London during the late summer of 1819. At this time he published *A Bill of Free and Sure Defence: or, an Act For a Constitutional Revival of the County Power, or Proper Militia of the Realm.* It was an elaboration of the scheme for national defence laid down in *England's Aegis* in 1806 and dealt in vague terms with the problem of drawing a militia from the entire community so that incidents like Peterloo

[1] *The Times*, 19 August 1819 [p. 3]; *The History of the Times, 'The Thunderer' in the Making 1785–1841* (New York, 1935), pp. 235–6, 238–9. See Bamford, *Passages in the Life of A Radical* for an eyewitness account. Two recent accounts, Robert Walmsley, *Peterloo: The Case Reopened* (Manchester, 1969) and Joyce Marlow, *The Peterloo Massacre* (London, 1969), differ in their apportionment of blame for the incident. A front-page review in *The Times Literary Supplement* (11 December 1969) demonstrates that passions have not died out.

could be avoided. Rhetorical, even by Cartwright's standards, and unusually (if naturally) bitter the pamphlet denounced 'These children of selfishness, these mole-eyed politicians' who caused a massacre of peaceful citizens seeking their rights.[1]

The events of 16 August 1819 angered those persons whose sense of justice was not blinded by fear and class prejudice. The government, however, continued to see evidence of sedition and would soon bring forward the notorious Six Acts. Meanwhile, in the autumn, Cartwright continued to be active despite the threat of prosecution which arose from the Birmingham meeting. On 12 November twelve resolutions prepared by him were adopted at a meeting of the Middlesex Freeholders which had been assembled to consider Peterloo. He also addressed a circular letter to several noblemen with respect to the conduct of the magistrates and yeomanry cavalry.[2] Nothing resulted from these efforts, which were not calculated to soothe the government into forgetting the prosecution. With Lord Sidmouth as Home Secretary, the Liverpool administration sometimes held the threat of a political trial over the head of an individual like a sword of Damocles, which it could drop at its pleasure. In March 1820 Cartwright realized that he was in danger and began to send *subpoenas* to persons whose evidence he thought might be useful.

The seventy-nine-year-old Cartwright's efforts on his own behalf were energetic and his mind lucid and fully aware of what was at stake. He was, in fact, more to the point in arranging his defence at the forthcoming trial than in discussing constitutional and legal matters in the abstract. The task of someone in Cartwright's position is to demonstrate the respectability, even triteness, of his views. This Cartwright endeavoured to do by corresponding with former associates in reform, some of whom he had not seen in years, to gain testimony that he, far from conspiring against the constitution, had laboured to prevent its overthrow. He then attempted to secure a fair jury. Here his

[1] *A Bill of Free and Sure Defence*, etc. (London, 1819), preface. As an example of the rhetoric: 'On their [the people's] side are God and nature, the laws and constitution of their country, the powers of reason, truth, and justice: against them only corruption and the sword...'

[2] *L and C*, vol. II, p. 174.

protest against selecting only esquires to be jurymen was disallowed and the practice of packing juries in cases like this was not discontinued until the Home Secretaryship of Sir Robert Peel.

On 22 March Cartwright, accompanied by his wife and niece, arrived at Warwick. The effort proved fruitless for the trial had to be postponed due to the illness of the judge. After a visit to Samuel Parr, 'the Whig Dr. Johnson', and an examination of Warwick Castle, the three travellers returned to London. They arrived there on 7 April 'after a fortnight of unavailing anxiety, expense and trouble...'.[1]

The delay was only temporary. On 3 August the trial began at Warwick with Baron Richards presiding. The account given by Cartwright's niece differs in several respects from that provided by Wooler's *Black Dwarf*. Miss Cartwright was anxious to show her uncle as a lofty, Jove-like figure who disdained attempting to secure his acquittal, preferring instead to use the trial as a means of instructing the entire nation in his constitutional principles. Cartwright, however, was not aloof from reality, and while he refused to sacrifice his ideals he made a vigorous defence of his actions.[2] He made a mistake when, perhaps acting upon the advice of others, he refused to allow witnesses to be called in his defence. Only Wooler was his own attorney; he spoke for three-and-three-quarter hours. Cartwright's defence was read by his solicitor and took four or four-and-a-half hours. In printed form it runs to 135 pages. The verdict might have been foreseen; after only twenty minutes' deliberation the jury declared the defendants guilty of seeking to sow hatred and contempt of the government in the peoples' minds.

On 29 May 1821, Cartwright and the others were called up for judgment. As originally offered, an affidavit from Cartwright began by impeaching the justice of the special jury practice, but when this was disallowed it was altered to assert that Cartwright

[1] *Ibid.* p. 183. In his *Dr. Parr, A Portrait of The Whig Dr. Johnson* (Oxford, 1966), Warren Derry says that Parr was not at home when Cartwright stopped by but commiserated with the Major by letter. See p. 327.

[2] *Ibid.* pp. 187–96. The entire 9 August 1820 issue of the *Black Dwarf* is devoted to a description of the trial. Also, the *Annual Register*, vol. 62 (1820 – Part II) has a succinct account. See pages 958–61.

did not conspire at Birmingham to overthrow the government but instead used his best efforts to restore and renovate the constitution. He asked for imprisonment rather than a fine as his income consisted almost entirely of a modest annuity. A severe fine would disinherit his niece. Denman, the renowned Whig barrister, who had recently acted as Solicitor General to Queen Caroline, attempted to show that Cartwright's appearance on the hustings at Birmingham was accidental, and spoke of the peaceful nature of that assembly and the splendid character of Cartwright. After hearing solicitations for the other defendants the court deliberated about half-an-hour and then Mr Justice Bayley delivered sentence. Cartwright was fined £100, but Wooler was sentenced to imprisonment for fifteen months and also had to give securities for five years. Two other defendants, Edwards and Maddocks, were sentenced to prison terms of nine and eighteen months respectively. Cartwright immediately counted out £100 in gold from his purse, remarking that they were all 'good sovereigns'.[1]

Thus the prison term which might have been imposed was avoided and an unchastened Major Cartwright was free to pursue his reform activities. But in his lengthy defence at Warwick 'this venerable, this worthy and excellent man', as Denman called him, made a commendable effort. True to his attempt to demonstrate that he was a pillar of the constitution, not its destroyer, Cartwright cited his life-long efforts on behalf of the honour and glory of England. These included not only his work on behalf of political reform but, bearing in mind the prejudices of the jury, the plans for a temple of naval celebration. He did not shrink from describing the state of politics. Indeed, the main point of his defence was the injustice of ignoring rotten boroughs while regarding the efforts of five men as subversive.[2] Afterwards he attacked unjust laws and statutes which had no foundation in reason or the divine law. From here he took his listeners through his career as a political agitator, noting associations with Jebb,

[1] *L and C*, vol. II, pp. 209–14.

[2] *A Defence, Delivered at Warwick, Third of August 1820, by Major Cartwright, Indicted in his Eightieth Year, For a Conspiracy against the Constitution* (London, 1831), p. 18.

Wyvill and other respectable leaders of reform and his role as a founder of the exclusive Friends of the People. In conclusion, he asserted that he did not know more than three or four persons who were present at the Birmingham meeting and that he was 'incapable of conspiring against that constitution which it has been the labour of my life to uphold'.[1] All in all, it was an impressive performance for an eighty-year-old man and was much less rambling than his usual efforts. Of course, as Dr Johnson once noted, a sentence of death concentrates the mind wonderfully, but it is impossible not to admire a man who could assert his principles in the face of a prison term that might have been the equivalent of a life-long sentence.

After the false alarm about a trial in March, Cartwright became involved in the cause of Caroline of Brunswick, George IV's wife, who was trying to gain recognition as England's rightful queen. The former Prince Regent instituted divorce proceedings to get rid of his wife whom he had not seen for a generation and to prevent her from being queen at the same time. Many Whigs and radicals, desperate for a means to embarrass the government, persuaded themselves that Caroline had not only been deprived of her position at the side of her husband but was the victim of a debauched libertine. Personal ambitions also played a role as Brougham, Denman and Alderman Wood saw a rare opportunity present itself to embarrass and even bring down the Tory government. Indeed, the constitutional issue often tended to get lost in the conflict of personalities, striving for political advantage and unsavoury details which were revealed about the private lives of both George and Caroline.[2] The frivolous and hedonistic Caroline and the moral and abstemious Cartwright were a remarkable contrast in personality and life style – even more so than the Queen and the bluff William Cobbett, who had returned to England in late 1819 and become a courtier kissing the hand of this gross woman.

Immediately after the end of his second trial in August Cartwright became more active in this effort. A long letter to the

[1] *Ibid.* passim.

[2] Halévy, *Liberal Awakening*, pp. 84–104.

Queen was published in the *Black Dwarf* and took the line of the reformers; it identified Caroline's cause with the peoples' desires and upheld parliamentary reform as the only salvation for the country. Cartwright compared her return to England with the coming of William of Orange in 1688, but noted that the latter event, which had promised so much, meant in the end a change for the worse as it fastened boroughmonger rule upon England. The letter also restated the old arguments in favour of political reform and a citizens' militia.[1] In the following month Cartwright, together with Hobhouse, Alderman Wood and Wooler presented an address of the Artisans, Mechanics and Labouring Classes of Manchester to Caroline, who stood while desiring the aged Major to sit. On 11 October Cartwright again appeared before the Queen. This time he was clad in the uniform of the Nottinghamshire militia, complete with buttons having the cap of liberty engraved upon them. He was accompanied by two of his fellow conspirators, Wooler and W. G. Lewis, and they presented to her majesty an 'Address of the Females of Manchester'. Before leaving, Cartwright also gave her a set of flags with mottos which favoured liberty.[2] In the end no one was satisfied. George did not get his divorce while Caroline, by accepting a government bribe of £50,000 a year and a house lost much of her popularity. The Tories looked poorly but their rule was not shaken. Nevertheless, the case of Queen Caroline was the most important political issue of the year 1820 and, sad to say, was more successful in expressing resentment against reaction than many a worthy cause.

One such movement presented itself in the revolt in Spain led by Rafael de Riego y Nuñez against the despotic and incompetent rule of King Ferdinand VII. Cartwright's enthusiasm for Spanish liberalism was as intense as his knowledge of Spanish history and traditions was limited. Before his second trial he exclaimed: 'Let the tyrants do what they will at Warwick – I am ready to encoun-

[1] *Black Dwarf*, 6 September 1820, pp. 341–51. The letter was dated 14 August – just ten days after Cartwright's trial at Warwick ended.

[2] *Black Dwarf*, 20 September 1820, p. 443; 18 October 1820, p. 551. Cartwright's niece clearly did not approve of Caroline for she scarcely mentions her uncle's actions on the Queen's behalf.

ter them. One Country has at any rate shaken off the shackles of tyranny – Spain is free!'[1] The judgment was as hopelessly optimistic as were his earlier pronouncements when Spain rebelled against the rule of Napoleon. He worked at promoting the inevitable public dinner, which was finally held on 2 October 1820, and continued to show interest in the cause of the Spanish liberals after their rebellion had been crushed by the machinations of the Continental members of the Quintuple Alliance.

Persons of generous and liberal sentiments joined him in expressing goodwill toward the Spanish revolutionaries. Many of them were also as irritated as he was at the activities of government paid *agents provocateurs* who continued trying to find nests of radicals and involve the members in seditious activities. The revulsion against Peterloo caught up both Whigs and radicals and the support for the revolution in Spain was broad based. There was no real cooperation, however, between the followers of Grey and men such as Hunt, Cobbett and Cartwright, who were considered beyond the pale of respectability. Whig historians to the contrary, even during the passage of the Six Acts at the end of 1819 'the Whigs occasionally made good speeches, but offered no really serious resistance'.[2] The record of the Whig parliamentary party during these momentous events was dismal.[3]

When J. G. Lambton, the future Earl of Durham, drew up a bill which provided for household suffrage and equal electoral districts, he hesitated to present it because of the opposition of the leaders of his Whig party. Cartwright was stung by this vacillation into demanding radical reforms. The latter 'speaks to the very souls of men', whereas moderate reform is 'spiritually cold and excites no generous emotion'.[4] Apart from showing Cartwright at his rhetorical worst, *A Letter to Mr. Lambton* is a measure of the gulf which separated even the respectable radicals who eschewed the use of physical force from those who were willing to accept limited change. Divinely sanctioned radical reform may have been, and government indeed may be, a science

[1] *Black Dwarf*, 10 May 1823, p. 643.

[2] The words in the quotation are by Graham Wallas. See *The Life of Francis Place*, p. 148.

[3] Mitchell, *Whigs in Opposition*, chs. 6 and 7.

[4] *A Letter to Mr Lambton* (London, 1820), pp. 2–3.

as Cartwright insisted but few of his countrymen could agree that 'The truths of the doctrine [universal male suffrage] leave no perplexing doubts in the mind...'[1] When Lambton finally mustered courage to present his bill it was quickly defeated in an almost empty House of Commons.

Within a few years several large and small issues had arisen upon which moderate and radical reformers could make common cause but on none was there a real joining of hands. Peterloo, for example, was denounced roundly from many sides yet there was no concerted effort to bring down the government which had condoned it. Personal jealousies and divided motivations wasted the opportunity presented by the claim of Caroline to be England's queen. The Riego revolt in Spain was perhaps too much removed from English affairs to excite more than a broad but unco-ordinated sympathy. The Liverpool government could therefore muddle along with the support not only of the boroughmonger faction but also of the rank and file of respectable opinion, which did not always approve of its policies but felt that in the rural shires and tranquil parsonages things might be a lot worse.

None of the political issues of the time was a threat to established Tory rule. The alliance of the propertied groups, however, was under strain. Dissatisfaction over the Corn Law of 1815, the determination of the government to pay off every penny of the national debt and Peel's policy of deflation were solid economic issues upon which a critique of the *status quo* could be based. Indeed, they did contribute to political change in the 1820s. Yet a feature of Cartwright's writings was his general non-involvement with economic problems. This was true even in the case of Peterloo, where he only attacked the obvious political repression and ignored the causes of the suffering which had led tens of thousands of people to congregate in St Peter's Fields. As he entered the final few years of his life, Cartwright possessed no more insight than he had as a former navy officer who adopted the cause of the American colonists.

Meanwhile, from his home at 37 Burton Crescent, to which he had moved in 1819 for the sake of his niece's health, Cartwright

[1] *Ibid.* p. 4.

continued his reform activities. He was the prime mover of a Middlesex County meeting which took place on 16 January 1821. Nine persons, including Cartwright, Jeremy Bentham, Burdett, Wood and Sir Charles Wolseley, were requested to form a council of guardians of parliamentary reform. Wolseley was one of the founders of the Hampden Club. He was also a good friend of Cartwright, and in 1819 it was while paying a visit to Sir Charles that the latter determined to visit the ill-fated Birmingham meeting. Of course, nothing resulted from this meeting or from several others which the Major attended while awaiting sentence after the verdict at Warwick. One protest meeting was rather different. It was held on 18 April with Cartwright in the chair and, with the question of Catholic Emancipation in mind, it denounced the union of church and state and held up as ideal the freedom and equality of religious denominations which existed in the United States. In this Cartwright modified his earlier attitude respecting the Catholics, which claimed that their equality could only come as part of a full-scale political reform.[1] But the eighty-year-old 'father of reform' had not changed his mind on the strictly political issues which lay closest to his heart.

[1] *L and C*, vol. II, pp. 22, 148, 208–9. *Black Dwarf* (25 April 1821), pp. 607–8.

CHAPTER 9

THE INDEFATIGABLE OCTOGENARIAN

William Hazlitt, who wrote as Cartwright entered the last few years of his life, poked fun at the Major in an essay entitled 'On People with one Idea'. The idea, of course, was political reform. 'Place its veteran champion under the frozen north, and he will celebrate sweet smiling Reform: place him under the mid-day Afric sun, and he will talk of nothing but Reform...' Cartwright must indeed have resembled 'a political homily personified' to the liberal Hazlitt, whose acid pen limned the defects of his contemporaries.[1] He was still incapable of innovation for tactical advantage beyond that which he had permitted himself a few years earlier under the guidance of Sir Francis Burdett. Perseverance along well established lines continued to motivate this upright, stubborn man.

Cartwright persisted in showing an active interest in the cause of liberty outside England and in searching as before for useful allies in domestic reform. One of these prospective allies was Joseph Hume, M.P. for Aberdeen. Hume was one of the small band of radicals in the unreformed House of Commons. A stolid man of great physical stamina but average intelligence, Hume was a leader of the contemporary agitation to repeal the Combination Acts and the legislation which prohibited the emigration of artisans and the export of machinery. Like almost everyone else of his political persuasion he advocated economy in government. He was renowned as a frequent talker and an observer claimed that Hume 'speaks more in the course of a Session than any other three members put together'.[2] Hume's endurance and patience made him an effective champion of radical causes and Cartwright tried to interest him in his own programme of reform. Four open letters in the *Black Dwarf*, personal corres-

[1] P. P. Howe (ed.), *The Complete Works of William Hazlitt* vol. 8 (London, 1931), pp. 59–61.

[2] [James Grant] *Random Recollections of the House of Commons*, etc. (London, 1836), p. 271.

pondence and at least one interview were the means by which Cartwright worked to get Hume to adopt his own form of political radicalism.[1] The two men were an unlikely pair to work together and Cartwright's attempt failed. Hume was an extreme example of English empiricism and found the Major's theories unappealing. At the same time the latter must have been vexed by Hume's absorption with financial and industrial questions.

While the fact was not explicitly stated, Hume had been cast in the role of the new radical champion, replacing Burdett. At the same time that he was courting Hume, Major Cartwright declined to attend a meeting in honour of Henry Hunt when the 'hero of Peterloo' was released from jail where he had spent the last two years. Cartwright's excuse was ill health but his personal activity belies this; Hunt's egocentrism and bluff manner annoyed many people besides Cartwright. He was certainly the most image-conscious radical politician of any importance. Actually, the two men had several points in common: a few simple political ideas tenaciously held, mediocre speaking ability (despite Hunt's sobriquet 'Orator') and personal good nature. Never really close, they now drew further apart and Hunt did not attend Cartwright's funeral or subscribe to the monument which was erected afterwards. Two other politicians, both orthodox Whigs, were approached by Cartwright in this same year. J. G. Lambton had agreed to the principles of taxpayer suffrage, triennial parliaments and the abolition of rotten boroughs. Cartwright naturally wanted him to adopt the four points which were now the essence of his own creed: universal male suffrage, equal electoral districts, annual elections and the secret ballot. He lectured Lambton on the principles of government without any result.[2] Shortly afterward he approached the young Lord John Russell, who had also won some notice as an advocate of parliamentary reform. This future Prime Minister was the last member of the Russell family whom Cartwright had, over the years, tried to interest in radical political change. In his numerous *Letters to Lord John Russell*,

[1] *Black Dwarf*, 29 August 1821, pp. 287–92; 12 September 1821, pp. 377–83; 19 September 1821, pp. 414–20; 3 October 1821, pp. 484–92. Also, *L and C*, vol. II, pp. 218–19.
[2] *Black Dwarf*, 7 March 1821, pp. 417–28; 28 March 1821, pp. 459–64.

Cartwright focused upon the large national debt and high taxes, both of which he blamed upon the political system.[1] Neither was discussed in relation to economic changes in the country; the debt and taxes were seen as aberrations which might be easily removed.

There were several exciting developments as Cartwright continued his support for overseas struggles against foreign or domestic oppressors. The 1820 liberal and national revolts won his instant sympathy and patriots in exile found the Old Major a ready source of advice and encouragement. In 1821 Cartwright wrote a military manual entitled *Hints to the Greeks* and three years later when he had only two months to live he actually drew up a constitution for a free Greece. This document, which was entitled 'A Suggestion Submitted to the Lawgivers of Greece', was English through and through. How else to account for the advice that the senate be replaced by a Witenagemot? Nor was Greece wholly in his mind when he called for a militia composed of all able-bodied men, juries drawn from the people as a whole, thrift in government, the separation of church and state and allowing no hereditary powers and privileges.[2] On the other hand, the 'Suggestion' may also be regarded as an expression of the sublime cosmopolitanism of the Enlightenment. It represented a belief that human beings had more in common than later generations, fed upon a ferocious nationalism, could possibly agree. Cartwright could not escape being touched by this feeling, though he was in so many ways out of touch with intellectual currents.

Spain was even more in his mind during these last few years. Since 1808 he had been actively concerned with affairs in the Iberian Peninsula and had warmly supported the Riego Revolt. Just a few months before the battle of the Trocadero brought an end to the revolt, Cartwright was pleased that his *Bill of Rights and Liberties* had been translated into Spanish but worried about difficulties experienced in electing members to the Cortes. He was much moved by the suffering of Riego and his family and

[1] *Black Dwarf*, 20 February 1822, pp. 283–8; 6 March 1822, pp. 358–60; 10 April 1822, pp. 533–40; 24 April 1822, pp. 603–11; 1 May 1822, pp. 640–7.

[2] *L and C*, vol. II, pp. 386–90.

designed a monument to the martyred Spanish liberal which was not accepted by the Royal Academy. Only an extreme cynic would assert that Cartwright's exertions to honour the dead Riego and to arrange for public meetings in support of this lost cause were motivated by a desire to strike a blow at England's rulers. As a compassionate, generous man he was deeply moved by events in Spain. When he was dying he took his pen in hand for the last time and wrote: 'It was Almighty God, who in forming Spaniards for such felicity, made them *men*. It was a succession of tyrants, who, for reducing them to slaves, made them cavaleros, hidalgos, grandees, and taught them the contemptible nonsense of family blood. Virtue alone is true nobility: patriot services for establishing common right and universal freedoms are alone legitimate titles to public trust and distinction.'[1] That there was a lesson intended here for England, Cartwright would not deny; we may see it as the testament of a decent and sincere individual.

The liberal revolt in Spain had repercussions in Mexico, where the tyrant Iturbide was made emperor by clerical and reactionary forces which feared the principles of Riego and his followers. Cartwright followed his usual course and advised the Mexican liberals about their future government. He lived long enough to receive thanks from one of them, Matteo Llanos Gutierez. While he was mortally sick he dictated a letter to General Michelena, the Mexican envoy in London, recommending a young officer whose talents might prove useful. When Cartwright learned of the deposition of Iturbide he exclaimed, 'I am glad, I am very glad!' These were almost the last words which he spoke.[2]

A new theme which attracted his attention after the trial arising out of the Birmingham meeting was the integrity of the jury system. While Cartwright had previously been content to insist upon juries being selected from the whole citizenry, he now came to regard the secret deliberation of the jury after a trial as evil. Since no guilty verdict could be delivered if one person clung firmly to a belief in the innocence of the accused, there was clearly no need for the jury deliberating. Instant verdicts after the trial would prevent this solitary juror from being coerced by the

[1] *Ibid.* p. 281. [2] *Ibid.* p. 283.

others. Here Cartwright was in danger of parodying himself, but the point rankled and he referred to it on several occasions.[1] It was connected with his growing belief in individual liberty of a nineteenth-century variety which had become clear in his 1818 *Letter to Sir Francis Burdett*. Also, perhaps this involvement with jury trials was an unconscious admission that the political reformers were a minority group.

At the age of eighty Cartwright's mind was as active as ever. Old associates, Horne Tooke, Earl Stanhope and Christopher Wyvill had died but the Major, 'that sternly honest, and amiably good man', as his friend Wooler called him[2] was very much alive. He had become more sensitive to criticism with increasing age, as his somewhat captious reproof of the jury system showed. A coarse reference in a scurrilous publication led him to sue the author for libel in April 1822. However, a legal technicality caused the suit to be dismissed in court and this considerably annoyed Cartwright.[3] A few months later a passing reference to 'the aging Cartwright' in a learned *Edinburgh Review* article that criticized some of the reformers for their thin knowledge of history led him to a ponderous but feeble reply in the *Black Dwarf*.[4] The Major's sense of humour flourished best around his fireside. Accumulated years of disappointment had taken their toll of his disposition and he was ill-equipped to deal either with the viciousness of *The Book of Wonders* or the erudition of the *Edinburgh Review*. Yet in this same year he registered disapproval

[1] *Black Dwarf*, 18 July 1821, pp. 100–8; 5 September 1821, pp. 341–6; 8 May 1822, pp. 661–4.

[2] *Black Dwarf*, 19 September 1821, p. 402.

[3] The issue involved a sentence in *The Book of Wonders* (London, 1821), an elaborate pamphlet which consisted entirely of a sustained attack upon Cobbett and had nothing to do with Cartwright. Cobbett's inconsistencies were frequently held up to ridicule by his enemies. *The Book of Wonders* quoted many of his remarks to show how frequently Cobbett changed position. The following sentence, which brought Cartwright's suit, was also included. 'The Major's letter thrust the point up to the hilt into the rascally Rump.' (Col. 46.) The rump was the faction within the Westminster Committee which supported Burdett, toward whom Cobbett now felt a great enmity. Although the alleged quote was supposed to be taken from volume 34 of the *Political Register*, which contains an open letter from Cobbett to Cartwright, it was a fabrication and does not appear. See *Political Register*, 5 December 1818, col. 324.

[4] *Edinburgh Review*, vol. XXXVI, 1 February 1822, pp. 288–341; *Black Dwarf*, 16 June 1822, pp. 849–62.

of Napoleon's conduct on St Helena with the remarks, 'There was a querulousness in the complaints of Buonaparte which was inconsistent with real greatness. I saw nothing of that dignity of mind which suffers in silence, and disdains complaint.'[1]

Despite these personal problems Cartwright was still busy as a writer. Some of his letters addressed to prominent personalities were printed in the *Black Dwarf* but he carried on personal correspondence also. He confided many of his thoughts to the versatile Thomas Northmore, who was interested in political developments and literature as well as applied science. Cartwright had no cultural interests whatever and his letters were concerned with politics. Even in the post-Peterloo doldrums, when the subject of reform was becalmed, Cartwright was as enthusiastic as ever. Nor did his fundamental views alter. The man who in 1821 noted that 'in first principles, on which all the rest depends, such a perfect agreement is natural to men of sense and integrity, who have paid an ordinary attention to the science of politics' was the same person who, in 1785, had referred to 'the science of civil government'.[2] An eight page pamphlet of 1821 called for the familiar universal male suffrage, annual parliaments and secret ballot. It also proposed a grass roots organization that was aimed at achieving parliamentary reform. Brotherhoods consisting of twelve persons apiece would be the nucleus of the organization. Three brotherhoods would form one trithing, six trithings one panel, two panels one fraternity, ten fraternities one vicinage and twenty vicinages would create the folkmote. This complex but democratic system was designed to circumvent the Six Acts of 1819, which placed great restrictions on public meetings.[3] The three specific recommendations for reform, plus one calling for equal electoral districts, were passed at a public meeting held in Hackney this same year.[4] Neither of these efforts met with the slightest success.

In a letter printed in the *Black Dwarf* Cartwright reiterated his

[1] *L and C*, vol. II, p. 225.

[2] *L and C*, vol. II, p. 216; *The Postscript to Major Cartwright's Reply to Soame Jenyns Esq.* (London, 1785), p. 8.

[3] *Declaration of Principles* (London, 1821), passim.

[4] *L and C*, vol. II, p. 220.

argument for universal male suffrage, making special note of the fact that it was to include the poor.[1] Full participation in the franchise was about as much as Cartwright was willing to allow those living in poverty; he never had a plan to relieve economic distress. On the other hand, writing to George Birkbeck in 1823, Cartwright urged the founder of the Mechanics Institutes to permit the operation of this scheme which made scientific knowledge available to the working class to be in the hands of the workers themselves.[2] It was an unusual sentiment for a middle class reformer to hold. Founded as part of the 'March of Mind' movement, the Mechanics Institutes supplied lectures and reading rooms for the artisan class. They were also used to propagandize for middle class political and social values and in many cases gradually shifted to the provision of genteel literary fare for clerks.[3] Cartwright showed unusual prescience in recognizing in 1823, the year the first Mechanics Institute was founded in Glasgow and a year before the London Mechanics Institute was organized, that education along these lines would provide values as well as instruction. Nevertheless, while Cobbett, motivated by a similar awareness, poured scorn upon the Mechanics Institutes and their founder, Cartwright made a financial contribution to the cause.

Politics, however, absorbed most of his energies. He was as impatient as ever with Whiggish procrastination and remained adamant for radical political reform. Public meetings continued to have validity in his eyes, although he was well aware of the Whig tactic of using these meetings to pass a half-hearted resolution in favour of reform instead of one with radical principles. Since the specific measures of universal male suffrage, equal electoral districts, annual elections and the secret ballot had become the fundamental part of Cartwright's programme, they received a great deal of attention from him. Realizing that his time on earth was running out, he tried to leave behind these few simple precepts to guide the people. In February 1823 they were

[1] *Black Dwarf*, 27 June 1821, pp. 923–32. [2] *L and C*, vol. II, pp. 251–2.

[3] For a discussion of the Mechanics Institutes and their problems see J. F. C. Harrison, *Learning and Living 1790–1960, A Study in the History of the English Adult Education Movement* (Toronto, 1961).

moved by Cartwright at a Middlesex meeting for reform. When D. W. Harvey, a member of parliament who was considered to be rather radical, said that reform should be left to the House of Commons as far as degree was concerned, Cartwright replied that 'When you depart from principles, you open a wide door to corruption.'[1] Earlier, the Whigs had tried to get him to give up these resolutions for the sake of achieving unanimity behind more moderate ones. His resolutions, however, were carried by an almost unanimous vote.

In the petition which accompanied the resolutions Cartwright laid stress upon the evils of the funding system. Finance had never occupied his attention earlier but there was by 1823 a fairly widespread disgust over the government's fiscal policies. The war against France had upset Pitt's complicated scheme for keeping national expenditure within bounds. Government expenses rose from £26,200,000 in 1790 to £174,070,000 in 1813 and in 1815 the total debt (including debts incurred for the Emperor of Germany and for Portugal) was £832,197,004. Since the repeal of the income tax at the end of the war the burden of taxation (which had always been mainly indirect) fell even more heavily upon the poor. Meanwhile, the government never wavered in its determination to keep faith with the nation's creditors, even though such a policy meant that a debt which had been contracted in inflated paper would be paid off in coin. Through taxes and inflation the working classes were the chief sufferers from this policy, but many formerly well-to-do landowners suffered as well. In the early 1820s the latter were meeting and petitioning parliament for redress. To some sanguine individuals the time was ripe for an alliance between the landed proprietors, whose wealth had declined, and the common people. Such a union would be directed against holders of government securities.

Cobbett was one who tried to forge this alliance. He had long written on economic questions and felt that he knew more about this subject than anyone in the country. By 1823 he was insisting upon the repudiation of the national debt and the land-

1 'Proceedings of the Middlesex Meeting for Reform' (1823) in vol. 14 of Cartwright's *Works*, Houghton Library, Harvard University.

lords taking their place at the head of a union of all classes who lived on the land. Both policies were failures: the debt continued to be honoured by the landlord-dominated legislature and for their part most landowners relied upon the 1815 Corn Law to enable them to ride out the storm.[1] As his petition shows, Cartwright was clearly influenced by Cobbett's writings. He called for retrenchment in the form of abolishing sinecures, ceding all unprofitable foreign possessions, disbanding the standing army and economizing in the upkeep of the Church of England. Abolition of the debt was to be a last resort. The petition was ultimately presented in the House of Commons.[2] Cartwright's remedies in the petition were different from those which Cobbett chose but his rhetoric shows the bias of the Rural Rider. By the time this affair took place Cartwright was too old to be deeply affected by any new ideas and no doubt he saw in the financial crisis only an opportunity to press for political reform. It may be considered as one of his few digressions from a strictly political view of abuses in the state of the country. Unfortunately, it is also a reminder of the slender texture of his thought.

Shortly afterwards, Cartwright paid his last visit to Lincoln, the county where he had lived for so long. His original intention was to communicate in writing with a county meeting that was scheduled for the end of March. Age and infirmity had seemingly sapped his energy and he hoped that a petition could be prepared and carried without his presence. A long letter addressed to the meeting was written on 19 March 1823, but when Cartwright heard that there was no chance of his ideas being adopted in his absence he hastily made preparations to attend. Accordingly, the amazing octogenarian left for Lincoln with his niece and arrived in time to participate in the county meeting which was held on 26 March. The Whig, Sir Robert Heron, presented a conventional petition of his own in favour of moderate reform. Lincoln not being Middlesex, this petition easily won the support of the meeting over Cartwright's more radical views. His mission having

[1] The economic, political and social situation was very complex. For a discussion, see my *William Cobbett: His Thought and His Times*, chs. 8 and 9.

[2] *L and C*, vol. II, pp. 232–4.

failed, Cartwright returned to London with only the memory of a warm reception from his supporters to cheer him.[1]

On 19 May Cartwright wrote to the son of his former associate, Earl Stanhope, and argued that universal male suffrage would not mean anarchy as so many persons feared. His reasoning and examples of historical precedent were loose and unconvincing – clear evidence, one might have thought, that the elderly Major was losing his grip.[2] Surely no one could have suspected that the letter was merely an appetizer; the main course was not quite ready. When the *chef-d'oeuvre* did appear, it was perhaps Cartwright's masterpiece and drew enthusiastic praise from his friends. *The English Constitution Produced and Illustrated* consisted of 446 pages of political argument in the form of a dialogue between three persons. It was Cartwright's swan-song as a reformer but the document demonstrates no slackening of his mental powers. Dedicated to the political reformers of the United Kingdom, the book concentrated the work of a long lifetime in the service of radical reform. Cartwright was well aware that *The English Constitution Produced and Illustrated* was to be his last major effort. In the British Museum there is a letter from him to the librarian asking that this presentation copy be neatly bound so that the 'English People should be well acquainted with the Principles of the English Polity. . . .and contribute to render the English Constitution better understood than it has been.'

Most of the book is a reiteration of former arguments, but some points are made emphatically for the first time. For example, Cartwright states that there were no hereditary legislators in Anglo-Saxon times and that the House of Lords cannot be part of a free English government. This novel idea occupied only a few pages in a long book and was not central to his purpose in writing it. He goes on to assert that God makes men equal but kings make them unequal, and that not only should church and state be separated, but that Deism is desirable.[3]

In matters of religion Cartwright was a man of the eighteenth

[1] *Ibid.* vol. II, pp. 235–7. [2] *Black Dwarf*, 21 May 1823, pp. 731–41.
[3] *The English Constitution Produced and Illustrated* (London, 1823), pp. 185, 186, 231 392, 395.

century but he was never much affected by the 'magic of monarchy'. Holding few illusions about the Hanoverian kings, he simply became a bit more outspoken at this time. Even the gross and unpopular George IV was not singled out for special criticism; England's ills were too severe to be much affected by any occupant of the throne. Anglo-Saxon England naturally absorbed much of his attention. Denying Paine's view that England had no constitution, Cartwright admitted that the Anglo-Saxon constitution was unwritten but claimed that it was nevertheless an integral part of the people's lives. Yet when the Normans seized the country the absence of a written document made the imposition of aristocratic and ecclesiastical dominance easier. The barons at Runnymede were chided for not searching for the first principles of a constitution when they limited the power of King John.[1] The Bill of Rights of 1689 was likewise no substitute for a Constitution; it had not guarded the people's liberties.[2]

The essential point which Cartwright was labouring to make, and the crux of his later political thinking, was that there must be a distinction made between laws and constitution. The former are never part of a constitution for they are subject to amendment and repeal, whereas a true constitution was founded on eternal principles of nature. Paine therefore erred in identifying the constitution with the shifting standards of law. To Cartwright, a violation of the constitution would be more than a breach of law; it would mean committing an outrage upon every man's natural rights.[3] This point was made repeatedly.

The essentials of the English constitution were of course based on the Anglo-Saxon practices of a citizen militia and an elective legislature. As stated by Cartwright they amounted to five elements:

1 Those principles of truth and morality upon which liberty and social order depend.

2 A militia composed of all men capable of bearing arms.

3 A Witenagemot annually elected by the people for the purpose of enacting laws.

[1] *Ibid.* pp. vii, 9–11. [2] *Ibid.* p. 13. [3] *Ibid.* pp. 15–18; 77–80.

4 Grand and petit juries, fairly drawn, to apply the laws.

5 A magistracy elected by the people to perform executive duties.[1]

It was to achieve these goals that he had demanded universal male suffrage, annual parliaments, a secret ballot and equal electoral districts.

Cartwright's assumptions which lay behind these assertions were indicated in the text. The Anglo-Saxon constitution had been founded by Hengest, kings at that time were elected by the people, the rights of man derive from God through the laws of nature. Finally, the legislature, thoroughly subordinate to the constitution, is basically a functional body which has been elected to do a job.[2]

These were the main points of the book, but when not dealing with eternal issues, Cartwright advanced *obiter dicta* about the present. Colonists were necessary to carry freedom overseas and to form independent states as soon as they could protect themselves. Oppressed people in the older countries of Europe were to be aided in their struggles for freedom. As a political economist Cobbett was pre-eminent. Jews were an unhealthy influence in the state.[3] The aim of the book was to make the past a guide to the present and to prove that radical reform was not merely historically respectable but quite in line with the course of English development. Liberty was seen (and here the comparison with Burke arises once more) as an ancient and inalienable inheritance; it was the Englishman's birthright for the defence of his life and property. With a heart entirely English, Cartwright criticized Milton for favouring Greek and Roman models over native examples of liberty.

In effect, *The English Constitution Produced and Illustrated* was Cartwright's last will and testament to the nation and the views expressed in it were carefully considered. The reader turns reluctantly from a far-seeing and generous colonial policy and support of people fighting for liberty to dozens of pages of inaccurate historical analysis and dubious conclusions arising

[1] *Ibid.* pp. 85–6.

[2] *Ibid.* pp. 75, 85–7, 92, 147.

[3] *Ibid.* pp. 95, 99, 399, xvii.

from false premises. Unappealing in a different way was Cartwright's anti-semitism. While never expressed in the coarse terms of a Cobbett, it was founded on the same stereotype of the Jew as a man of commerce. It is noteworthy that Jews were not referred to in his earlier writings. Only when he became interested in financial questions did they appear. Perhaps the inspiration came from early eighteenth-century tracts but it is more likely that Cobbett's writings were the cause. An identification with business success was not generally popular with radicals either at this time or afterwards and left-wing elements on the Continent and in the United States were able to use Jews as scapegoats into the twentieth century. Personally the kindest of men, Cartwright was not always in touch with the civilizing and humanitarian impulses which were reducing bigotry in his society. Myopia on this issue was symptomatic of his often narrow view of human wants.

In cold print the inadequacies of Cartwright's theoretical equipment were revealed. So was his whimsical knowledge of history. A casual reference to the working classes makes clear both his constricted prospect of the social scene, and his weakness as a tactician in the art of practical politics. In this respect it can be put alongside his praise for the economic theory of William Cobbett. His book was privately printed and almost ignored by the journals of opinion. Later in the year Cartwright had several thousand medals struck on which were inscribed the five elements of genuine English policy that were stated in *The English Constitution Produced and Illustrated.*

In the same year in which Cartwright was performing prodigies of exertion on behalf of reform in England and abroad he found time to visit friends and relatives. His brother, Edmund, whose daughter had lived with the Major for many years, and whose invention of the power loom had caused him much expense and many anxious moments, died in October. John Cartwright himself had not long to live. The following February saw the last of his published writings. Called *A Problem*, it dealt with the union of all nations. The government of the United States of America 'in which the magnificent constitution of five-and-twenty sovereign states revolving round a sovereign congress' was to be the model for people everywhere. In this association of the nations there must be more than mere union; unanimity must be the goal. By following correct political principles this grand objective could be achieved and the chains of despotism thrown off.[1] The five principles of *The English Constitution Produced and Illustrated* were to be the elements of universal benevolence. Clearly, Cartwright's thoughts did not become more subtle with increasing age; rather he relied upon assumptions which had been proved in his mind much earlier. Although *A Problem* was shallow and naive, it does not show signs of mental decay. The Rousseauesque ideal of unanimity was the logical product of a fastidious man who liked tidy solutions to all problems. At eighty-three years of age Cartwright was as stubborn and satisfied with his own insight into political problems as the former naval officer who had taken up the cause of the American colonists half a century earlier.

The shortening of his daily walks were evidence of a weakening of the Major's physical powers and in the spring of 1824 he knew that he had not long to live. Cartwright's decline was gradual and peaceful. He diverted himself by distributing some of his books and naval equipment to relations whom he considered able to use them. It was also his wish that his body be dissected after death in a lecture for the benefit of medical students. The advocate of the *a priori* in politics had a strictly empirical view of the study of medicine. This instruction to his survivors was not obeyed.

His writings now consisted entirely of correspondence with domestic and foreign friends of liberty. In July he received a long letter from ex-president Thomas Jefferson of the United States. Jefferson expressed appreciation for the copy of *The English Constitution Produced and Illustrated* which Cartwright had sent to him. Like Cartwright the great Virginian had been misled into believing that in Anglo-Saxon times the kings called assemblies of the whole people; for the rest he had an agreeably Whiggish view of English political development. The letter is an excellent

[1] *L and C*, vol. II, pp. 391–5.

piece of Jeffersonian democracy. It closed with the touching words, 'Your age of eighty-four, and mine of eighty-one years, ensure us a speedy meeting. We may then commune at leisure, and more fully, on the good and evil, which in the course of our long lives, we have both witnessed; and in the mean time, I pray you to accept assurances of my high veneration and esteem for your person and character.'[1] The receipt of this letter was a high point in Cartwright's life. No Englishman in such a prominent position had ever paid him this honour.

Yielding to his family's belief that a change of air might relieve his steady fever, Cartwright allowed himself to be moved to Hampstead on 10 September, but as his condition worsened he was brought back to Burton Crescent on the sixteenth. There, on 23 September, he died. In accordance with his instructions the funeral was simple, the service being conducted by the rector of Finchley. In addition to his family several of his associates in reform attended. These included Thomas Wooler, who devoted the entire issue of 1 October 1824 *Black Dwarf* to Cartwright's death. Also attending were the Spanish martyr Riego's brother and General Pepe, the hero of the Neapolitan revolt of 1820 against the decrepit Bourbon dynasty.[2]

Several of Cartwright's former friends proposed that a public monument be erected to his memory and in June 1825 a meeting was convened at the Crown and Anchor Tavern with this purpose in mind. Sir Francis Burdett took the chair and eulogized Major Cartwright, dwelling mainly upon his patriotism, unselfishness and constancy of character. Others also spoke in testimonial of Cartwright.[3] These men were of the moderate reform group in parliament (John Cam Hobhouse and Alderman Wood, for example) and their dominance in the proceedings was an ironic commentary upon the work of the man to whose memory they desired to pay homage. Cartwright, who was adamant against compromise of principle throughout most of his career had failed to create a sizable faction of his own. The tiny physical

[1] *Ibid.* p. 275. The letter is quoted in its entirety by Cartwright's niece. It was forwarded proudly by the old man to Jeremy Bentham.

[2] *L and C*, vol. II, pp. 289–90; *Black Dwarf* (1 October 1824).

[3] *L and C*, vol. II, pp. 291–8.

force group had gone underground after the punishment of the Cato Street conspirators. His natural allies, Hunt and Cobbett, were temporarily in eclipse. He had alienated Francis Place and Joseph Hume by the narrowness of his vision, and these men had just successfully carried through parliament the repeal of the Combination Acts. The literary radicals were too fastidious. The working class was not, perhaps, fastidious enough. Thus he was left with the posthumous support of men whom he could never, while alive, coax into the type of political position which he demanded.

On 20 July 1831 a bronze statue by George Clarke was erected in Burton Crescent nearly opposite the house in which Cartwright died.[1] It resembles Houdon's statue of Voltaire, though without the sardonic smile which was placed upon the face of the sage of Ferney. By this time the Whigs were in power and prospects for limited reform were good. There was justification for a meeting of reformers at the White Conduit Tavern that day both to toast political reform and to honour the character of the late Major Cartwright. Had he been alive Cartwright would have been pleased that a measure of what he had so strongly urged was to be achieved, though its attenuated form might have excited him to cry, 'No compromise!' 'Stand fast by principle!'

[1] On 30 June 1908 Burton Crescent was renamed Cartwright Gardens.

CHAPTER 10

CONCLUSION: THE FATHER OF REFORM

In *The Comparison*, which was published in 1810, Cartwright claimed that 'All systems founded in the laws of nature, the work of the Deity, are simple; that is, ultimately resolvable into a few self-evident Principles.'[1] In this statement we have 'The Father of Reform' at his most characteristic: expressing a hard-won political philosophy with the greatest self-confidence. Such assurance is the mark of both the autodidact and the ideologue and certainly Cartwright fitted into each category. In the history of English political thought one finds examples of people who shared Cartwright's self-confidence, for example, those bores of the New Model Army who vexed Oliver Cromwell with their homespun dogmas. There were also the theorists who later clung to the fringes of the Labour Party – individuals whom H. G. Wells and George Orwell excoriated. While differing among themselves, these persons shared a belief in 'self-evident' truths.

What saves Cartwright from the harshest strictures was not his undoubted perseverance or personal integrity, for these qualities have been possessed by thoroughly evil men as well as by good ones. Nor was his humanitarianism, which was highly praised by his relatives and friends, as deep and far reaching as it might have been. By the standards of his own time his insensitivity toward physical suffering caused by economic distress and the genteel anti-semitism of his later days must be found wanting. He might indeed weep with emotion when reading about noble principles in a book, but it remains a fact that first-hand contact with misery did not shake him out of his complacent fixation on political principles. What is most noteworthy about the man is his anticipation of certain ideas such as universal male suffrage, equal electoral districts, the secret ballot and single member constituen-

[1] *The Comparison*, p. 30.

cies, which were to prove the means of bringing full political participation to future generations of Britons. He adopted these ideas early and clung to them through a life marked by political loneliness and frustrated ambition. Others shared with Cartwright the hope of achieving several of these objectives, but none of them went as far as he did or had so long a career. Here his personal qualities of decency and moderation which led him to avoid personal feuds at a time of vitriolic writing and caricature, may be seen to proper advantage: in support of principles which were to win eventual near-unanimous recognition. In a curious way, Cartwright, who scorned so many Whig politicians and broke with the Whig Club, was an embodiment of the Whig theory of history. His passionate concern for England more than any strictly intellectual accomplishment was probably responsible for his absorption of the spirit, if not the factual reality, of the course of English history and allowed him to contribute to others becoming what he was himself: a free-born Englishman.

These personal qualities were attractive to his contemporaries, though they did not enable him to win elective office. Nevertheless, the Major was respected by his associates and deservedly has achieved a larger niche in history than several of the latter who possessed a greater intelligence. His current reputation naturally rests mainly upon his political philosophy since he never served in parliament and was not a success during his lifetime as an inspirer of others. This emphasis upon Cartwright's ideas is also made necessary because his books and pamphlets are marked by an absence of that topicality which would render them of much value to the modern historian of his times. Discussion in such general principles as Cartwright employed makes for frustration if one is used to searching in the revealing writings of such contemporaries as William Cobbett, Thomas Creevey or Leigh Hunt. While comparisons with great political philosophers are vain, Cartwright must be seen through his writings and not merely as an amiable reformer who worked well with others who held similar views.

Cartwright's approach to politics was succinctly stated in *The First Address to the Public from the Society for Constitutional*

Information, which he wrote in 1780. Here it was immediately asserted that 'In the venerable Constitution handed down to us, through a long succession of ages, from our Saxon and British ancestors, this is the basis and the vital principle – LAW, TO BIND ALL, MUST BE ASSENTED TO BY ALL.'[1] From *Take Your Choice!* of 1776 until he died this sentiment, the self-evidence of which admitted no equivocation, was at the root of his political belief. Implied in it are the bases of his policy: a vision of the continuity of English history, absorption in domestic political affairs, and a belief in the essential simplicity of the principles and methods of government.

The looseness of thought which marked Cartwright's references to the English past is doubly vexing to the reader, for the views which he asserted were presented in a calm, matter-of-fact manner which assumes instant acceptance and therefore does not trouble to explain details. Cartwright saw English developments (Scottish and Irish affairs were seldom mentioned) as a consistent chain of events in which the present was linked with the past. National liberty might indeed be only the sum of the liberties of individual men, as he admitted in 1818. But the constitution was different from the laws which existed at any given moment. Indeed, the English constitution had been founded upon the laws of nature. Violations done to it were therefore infringements upon every man's material rights, and they had to be removed if England was once again to be free. Fortunately, this could be done peaceably by legislation.

Like other reputed radicals at the time, Cartwright at heart wanted to restore an earlier England. Sweeping away borough-monger corruption would help to accomplish this aim, but exactly what was England to revert to? Here his writings, seemingly so clear-cut about the past, are sometimes confusing. The virtues of the Anglo-Saxon militia were spelled out consistently and this subject provides no problem. The same is not true, however, of the ideal civil constitution. In *The People's Barrier* (1780) and *The Commonwealth in Danger* (1795) he first implied and then

[1] Wyvill's *Political Papers*, vol. 2, p. 465.

asserted the fact that England was basically a republic. The theme was never developed, although a year before he died he did strike out once more at kings in general.[1] In contrast to the loving and lavish detail accorded to the topic of a citizen militia the idea of a republic was left dangling. One can assume that this was only done in part for tactical reasons. In a similar fashion, he waited until the end of his life before advocating strenuously the separation of church and state and asserting in *The English Constitution Produced and Illustrated* that the House of Lords can never be part of a free English government. These latter views do not jibe with his earlier acceptance of England's medieval heritage. Cartwright, as we shall see, loved the past and only at the end of a frustrated career did he lash out at certain institutions. He was by no means a radical who wanted to uproot the past.

It must be mentioned once again that Cartwright was not as inflexible about tactics as some have alleged. We have witnessed his submission to Burdett on the question of a householder suffrage and his involvement with the ideas of other people through the Hampden Clubs. Evidence exists that as early as 1798 he was willing to adopt something less than universal male suffrage in order to get reform. At that time he praised Fox's advocacy of a uniform household franchise for the boroughs in this Whig's famous speech in the House of Commons during the preceding year. Cartwright urged Wyvill to support the same principle.[2] His failure as a politician was not entirely due to a refusal to bend for the sake of accommodating others.

That belief in the self-evidence of political truth and the consequent simplicity of government was perhaps the factor which most irritated his contemporaries and makes him appear as a faintly ridiculous figure in history.[3] The myth of Anglo-Saxon England which fascinated him was also irrelevant to the English people at the time, and there is something both pathetic and exasperating about a man who ignored reality in pursuit of a mythopoeic society. Cartwright sometimes reminds one of a

[1] *The English Constitution Produced and Illustrated*, p. 231.

[2] Wyvill's *Political Papers*, vol. 5, pp. 398–402, 405–9.

[3] White, *Waterloo to Peterloo*, p. 131.

naïf – a natural innocent in these matters – like Mrs Birdseye in Henry James' *The Bostonians*. He was indeed a poor public speaker and not much of a practical politician. Exclusion from parliament was the penalty which he paid for these and other failings. The ingenuousness of his ideas was of a piece with their creator: plain, simple and unaffected. While not entirely devoid of a capacity for compromise and able to produce an occasional home truth about a specific abuse he could seldom move others to wholehearted agreement. Integrity combined with perfect assurance produce a feeling of awkwardness and even resentment among colleagues when specific ideas seem out of focus.

Simplicity also accounts in large measure for Cartwright's ignoring economic and social events. Here, however, one must acknowledge that he shared this tendency with virtually all of his contemporaries, including those in charge of the government. He nevertheless failed to understand both the plight of the poor and the nature of the Industrial Revolution. Except on political grounds he had nothing to offer those who were suffering from poverty. Perhaps he believed that when England's ancient constitution was restored poverty would cease, though an examination of his writings does not sustain such an optimistic view. Certainly he had no social programme. It would appear that in this respect, too, Cartwright was a man of his times. Unconsciously believing that poverty was incapable of being eradicated, he gave no thought to the subject, but like his well-to-do associates stressed the sanctity of private property and saw only a minimal role for government in the life of the citizen.

The Industrial Revolution offered an opportunity to reduce poverty; Cartwright saw in it only a chance for his talented elder brother, Edmund, to make money. The same process would ensure that English government would grow more complex and expensive as it became of necessity a force which affected people's lives. The meliorative and positive results of industrialization for the people of Great Britain were invisible to Cartwright, but so were hardships for groups such as the Luddites and some of the people whom he met on his Hampden Club travels. Politics, in the form of 'the established maxims of civil government' was the invariable salvation of all difficulties. No aspect of Cartwright's career poses more problems for his admirers than does the myopia which affected his social vision even after his tours of the Midlands and North began in 1812.

Still, it has been noted that many others shared this short-sightedness with him, and there is perhaps no reason to single Cartwright out in this respect. This is true even though he was absorbed in domestic affairs which might have brought home certain truths to him. To do Cartwright justice, discussion of his merits and defects should properly centre around his chosen field of politics. The real question is how well did he understand objective political reality and how effective was he in acting upon his information? We have mentioned his advocacy of principles which would later become part of British political behaviour, as well as his personal shortcomings as a politician. Yet there is also the question of the political condition of England and Cartwright's relation to it.

Cartwright, of course, rejected the eighteenth-century constitution which had been derived from the post-1688 settlement. The delicate but unwritten relationship between the two branches of government and pocket boroughs, placemen and sinecures were not calculated to win his admiration. Believing that the constitution and the country's laws should be kept separate, Cartwright's brand of common sense could not accept a constitution which was a collection of written and unwritten laws. This was too unwieldly, too open to interpretation by lawyers (a class which he hated). The constitution should be understood by ordinary men.[1] Blind reverence for the past was certainly not his way. The five elements of *The English Constitution Produced and Illustrated* represented the essence of the English constitution as he saw it in his later years: universal male suffrage, annual parliaments, the secret ballot and equal electoral districts were the means by which they could be achieved. Both means and ends reflected established practice.

Of the five principles, the first, which referred to truth and morality upon which liberty and social order depend, was a

[1] *An Appeal*, p. 12.

cliché that said nothing specific. Another, reliance upon a militia of all men capable of bearing arms, seems just a piece of wishful thinking curious in a military man; it would have been useless in an age of professional armies and technology. The principle of an annually elected legislature was quietly forgotten by political theorists sometime after Cartwright's death and no one in the modern world of mass public opinion relishes the thought of perpetual election campaigns. Cartwright's desire for fairly drawn juries was achieved shortly after his death, but his last point in favour of an elected 'magistracy' was nebulous and we cannot be sure that he really wanted to end kingship. Nevertheless, his specific means have been generally proved to have merit. Again, annual elections (a means and an end for him) has been discarded as a goal. Cartwright is thus a more considerable figure than he appears to be if one is concerned only with his objectives, and his proposals to effect change are intelligible.

His life-long search for allies was due both to the means which he adopted (held to be extreme by virtually anyone with real power) and the ends, which confused persons who had their own ideas about what England needed in the way of political change. Cartwright's pleas to all sorts of persons, from the Prince Regent on down, to take the initiative in reform are at once pathetic and fatuous. No one stayed with him for any length of time. However self-effacing he was to his equals, Cartwright's constant exhortations to keep up to the mark must have been galling to those who also felt that some change was needed. To these men, the Major's opinions were not as obviously the proper way to achieve what was necessary as they were to their originator. Wyvill, Cobbett, Place and Burdett all had visions of what England should be and how this might be achieved. These men liked Cartwright but could not accept either his remedies or even on occasion his tactics. The latter, especially public meetings and petitions, with which Cartwright's name is most closely associated, had no chance of success in the England of his lifetime. His early colleagues in reform such as Wyvill grew weary and dropped by the wayside. Place and Burdett were willing to settle for moderate reform. Cobbett searched restlessly during the 1820s for new keys to open the doors of change but Cartwright remained faithful to the old principles. Like his contemporary, the artist Benjamin Robert Haydon, he was too convinced of his own rightness to adapt to others and paid the penalty of isolation.

Yet by a rather cruel oversight, Cartwright, who was ignored in his lifetime, has never received credit for his legacy which influenced Chartism and other reform movements. Too often the famous six points in the Chartist programme (universal male suffrage, annual elections, the secret ballot, equal electoral districts, abolition of property qualifications for members of the House of Commons, and payment of these members) have been regarded as indigenous to the working class instead of stemming from eighteenth-century gentleman reformers. Ironically, if middle-class England ignored Cartwright, the working classes adopted his views, and this came about at a time of heightened class consciousness on the part of the latter. The Chartists themselves paid tribute to him when they noted that 'the first attempt. . .to induce the people to concur in efforts to obtain a radical reform of the Commons House of Parliament was made by the late Major Cartwright'.[1] Cartwright's concentration upon politics, pride in England's past and strict avoidance of violence were factors which impressed later generations and helped to create a tradition of reform that owed little to foreign inspiration. As Bagehot noted, the English are a deferential people, and truly the history of politics in the nineteenth century bears out this observation.[2]

Thomas Paine, who won great *réclame* in England and France for a few years during the 1790s before returning to the United States and an obscure death in 1809, represented a strand of thought which never sank deep roots into the uncongenial English soil. Jacobinism as a theory was too iconoclastic, in practice too violent, to win substantial support. Like Marxism of a later date it smacked of the foreign and could not win the allegiance of the thoroughly xenophobic English working class. This group much

[1] *Address of the Metropolitan Reform Association* (1842). Quoted in *A History of the Chartist Movement* (New York and Boston, 1920) by J. West. See pp. 1–2.

[2] A. P. Thornton, *The Habit of Authority, Paternalism in British History* (London, 1965), chs. 4 and 5.

preferred the robust principles and surface common sense of a Cobbett, whose lively, topical articles appealed to the ordinary man's feelings about social justice in his native land.

Cartwright could also touch these men but not in the direct fashion of Cobbett. It is doubtful whether very many of them read his writings, despite the affection in which the Old Major was held during his Hampden Club tours. At a time when most of the poor were illiterate and a man who could read a newspaper might be regarded as a scholar by his working-class fellows, Cartwright's style and subject-matter would be obstacles to understanding. His highly speculative works made few concessions to the reader. Nor was their style particularly lucid. It was only in the fact that his writings were concerned with the English experience that he could appeal to the working class.

Cartwright's ideas were at large in the early nineteenth century. Many of them found expression in that considerable section of the newspaper press which addressed itself to poor and politically unrepresented Englishmen (Wooler's *Black Dwarf* was the most conspicuous example). There was no common point of view for these journals to follow; John Wade's *Gorgon* was particularly impatient of Cartwright's antiquarianism. Other papers had axes to grind of an economic or social nature. Some complied with the severe government tax upon periodicals while others went under ground and were published illegally. However, Cartwright's remedies for the sickness of England's constitution won wide acceptance among the publishers of radical newspapers and some of them would emerge as the Chartist programme in 1836.

Although none of Cartwright's writings had the immediate effect which he desired, they did enter into what his critic, Hazlitt, called 'The Spirit of the Age'. Alone of the reformers of his early years he lived long enough and had sufficient vitality and interest to propagandize his ideas in person during that period around Waterloo when public opinion was fast becoming an important force in political life. This circumstance assured him of permanent recognition while John Jebb and James Burgh are largely forgotten. In an age when many educated men believed that English political liberty had originated in Anglo-Saxon times, Cartwright's wholehearted faith in the liberty of pre-Norman society did not seem altogether ridiculous. In far away America his correspondent, Thomas Jefferson, had tried to learn the Anglo-Saxon language. This English background was reassuring to Cartwright's followers. Even when he was supporting efforts toward independence and freedom in the old and new worlds the thought of England was always present.

Cartwright the agitator and Cartwright the prolix pamphleteer cannot be separated. Those dozens of Addresses, Letters and Declarations were the foundation of his work – Cartwright himself might say they *were* his work. Nevertheless, he delivered many speeches. But these speeches and peregrinations in the countryside while he was in his seventies were secondary. Indeed, the Major insisted upon getting a speech down on paper and publishing it whenever he could. His speeches and travels were thus extensions of his real employment, which took place in his study. With a serene temper and a seldom shaken courage, he pursued his obstinate way through many years of frustration. Cartwright died in the middle of a decade which saw much change in economic, legal and religious matters. Legislation on these subjects helped prepare the way for the most important law to be enacted since the Glorious Revolution: the Great Reform Bill of 1832. The work of his lifetime was frequently scorned or neglected but he had wrought more cleverly than he knew. Cartwright's political agitation has a place in that climate of opinion which was to shape the future development of British life.

This legacy represents Cartwright's obvious contribution to the progress of political change. It was an appropriate bequest from a man who never escaped from the political and social milieu of his early days. Truly that environment must have been remarkable for it permanently captivated almost all members of his own and the next two generations. Rich and well placed individuals such as Liverpool and Castlereagh (both of whom were nearly thirty years younger than Cartwright) might well in their unimaginative ways have expressed a preference for the old over the new. But how to account for Wyvill and Cobbett?

'Hold fast by the laws', Major Cartwright exhorted his followers. In one way or another all of his colleagues in radicalism said the same thing. The faith of these men in the capacity of old English institutions had been implanted in them during their youth. Age and experience never really shook it, although there were moments of intense irritability when monarchy and the House of Lords came under hostile scrutiny.

Looking at Cartwright's long career one is impressed by how greatly it cleaved to the prevailing value system. Persons in government and Tory squires and parsons might denounce him as a radical agitator and see little difference between Cartwright and the miniscule group of physical force advocates of change, but they had mistaken their man. This error arose not merely because Cartwright wanted the restoration of what he imagined to be old forms of government but because most of his outlook was conservative. Certainly, his faith in reason and tendency to talk in the abstract have not been generally considered marks of the conservative thinker. However, beneath these surface attributes, which a person of such limited education could acquire from the baggage train of the Enlightenment, lay a personality steeped in order and tradition. Cartwright valued liberty rather than equality and believed in the natural law, which always hovered unexamined around his writings.

Major Cartwright may be seen as part of a rich tradition solidly rooted in native English values. Like Bolingbroke, whom he professed to dislike, he looked at politics from the point of view of the landed gentry who considered themselves to be the true representatives of England against the greedy, deracinated commercial interests which had created the national debt and paper money and did so much to corrupt political life. Love of country, duty, a reverence for the past, were enduring qualities which he represented. His brother's involvement in industrial technology was clearly a closed book to him but family loyalty, as well as his respect for private property, dictated his support. This was Cartwright's only substantial concession to the new business-oriented values. Otherwise, he represented that part of the squirearchy which took the minority position on public issues.

Cartwright's dislike of lawyers, and support of Cobbett's attacks upon commercial interests which were threatening the dominance of landed groups in the early 1820s, were part of this attitude and had he lived longer no doubt his general political argument would have been broadened. When Cartwright was a very old man these landed groups were threatened again by the government fiscal policy which arose out of the war against France. He himself had by 1820 an income which consisted almost entirely of an annuity. It is indeed tempting to think that if, on the basis of social symptoms which existed before he died, Cartwright could have predicted the direction in which English life was to turn increasingly after 1832, he might have rejected his own work.

Cartwright was a living link between the eighteenth and nineteenth centuries. When he died in 1824 only Jeremy Bentham, who was eight years younger than Cartwright, could claim a career of such continuity and Bentham was not directly involved in the world of politics. Cartwright was a spokesman for that portion of the old landed interest which was outraged by what it imagined to be unwelcome innovations in the constitution rather than a spokesman for the new democracy. This helps to explain his backward-looking politics. It was his great misfortune that the French Revolution created fear of change in his natural supporters and that the sequel to events in France was war between that country and England which intensified that fear to the point of paranoia. Furthermore, while the war created suffering in some quarters which had no political power, it produced a general but short-lived prosperity among those landed groups which might unwillingly have proven receptive to his programme if their economic interests had been badly hurt.[1] Thus in two respects the French Revolution deprived him of support for over a generation.

History is hard on those who are active during the wrong time. Cartwright's reputation as a well-meaning bore was not entirely undeserved, but he represented what might have been a more substantial opinion if events over which he had no control did not intervene. We may see him as the last reformer of the eighteenth-century stamp to survive until the threshold of a new age.

[1] After the war these groups placed their faith in the 1815 Corn Law to restore prosperity.

SELECTED BIBLIOGRAPHY

Cartwright's was an age of unusually temperamental journalists and factious reformers; references to him were often misleading. Perusal of his writings, therefore, is the only way to do justice to him. While there is no complete collection of these writings, the Houghton Library of Harvard University, the British Museum and the New York Public Library all possess substantial holdings.

The following list of books and articles is confined to those which have been cited in the text.

BOOKS

Anon., *A Winter's Evening's Conversation in a Club of Jews, Dutchmen, French Refugees and English Stockjobbers at a Noted Coffee House in Change Alley* (London, 1748).

The Book of Wonders (London, 1821).

The Extraordinary Black Book (new edition) (London, 1832).

The History of the Times. 'The Thunderer' in the Making 1785–1841 (New York, 1935).

The Jockey Club; or a Sketch of the Manners of the Age, Part III (2nd ed.) (London, 1792).

Bamford, Samuel, *Passages in The Life of A Radical* (London, 1967 ed.).

Black, E. C., *The Association, British Extraparliamentary Political Organization, 1769–1793* (Cambridge, Mass., 1963).

Brown, P. A., *The French Revolution in English History* (London, 1965).

Cartwright, F. D., *The Life and Correspondence of Major John Cartwright* 2 vols. (London, 1826).

Christie, Ian, *Myth and Reality in Late Eighteenth-Century British Politics and Other Papers* (Berkeley and Los Angeles, 1970).

Wilkes, Wyvill and Reform, The Parliamentary Reform Movement in British Politics, 1760–1785 (London, 1962).

Cole, G. D. H., *The Life of William Cobbett* (London, 1925).

Cone, Carl, *Burke and The Nature of Politics: The Age of The American Revolution* (Lexington, Ky., 1957).

The English Jacobins (New York, 1968).

Davis, H. W. C., *The Age of Grey and Peel* (Oxford, 1964).

Derry, Warren, *Dr. Parr, A Portrait of the Whig Dr. Johnson* (Oxford, 1966).

Feiling, Keith, *The Second Tory Party, 1714–1832* (London, 1959).

[Grant, James,] *Random Recollections of The House of Commons* (London, 1836).

Halévy, Elie, *The Growth of Philosophic Radicalism* (Boston, 1960).
The Liberal Awakening, 1815–1830 (New York, 1949).
Harrison, J. F. C., *Learning and Living 1790–1960, A Study in the History of The English Adult Education Movement* (Toronto, 1961).
Howe, P. P. (ed.), *The Complete Works of William Hazlitt* (London, 1931).
Hunt, Henry, *Memoirs* (3 vols.) (London, 1820–2).
Kemp, Betty, *King and Commons, 1660–1832* (London, 1957).
Kramnick, Isaac, *Bolingbroke and His Circle* (Cambridge, Mass., 1968).
Maccoby, S., *English Radicalism, 1786–1832* (London, 1955).
Mantoux, Paul, *The Industrial Revolution in The Eighteenth Century* (London, 1961).
Marlow, Joyce, *The Peterloo Massacre* (London, 1969).
Mitchell, Austin, *The Whigs in Opposition, 1815–1830* (Oxford, 1967).
Morpurgo, J. E. (ed.), *The Autobiography of Leigh Hunt* (London, 1949).
Namier, Lewis, *England in The Age of The American Revolution* (2nd ed.) (London, 1961).
The Structure of Politics at The Accession of George III (2nd ed.) (London, 1961).
Osborne, John W., *The Silent Revolution: The Industrial Revolution in England as a Source of Cultural Change* (New York, 1970).
William Cobbett: His Thought and His Times (New Brunswick, 1966).
Patterson, M. W., *Sir Francis Burdett and His Times* (London, 1931).
Plumb, J. H., *The Growth of Political Stability in England, 1675–1725* (London, 1967).
Radzinowicz, Leon, *A History of English Criminal Law and its Administration from 1750*, vol. 1, *The Movement for Reform, 1750–1833* (New York, 1948).
Read, Donald, *Peterloo, The 'Massacre' and its Background* (Manchester, 1958).
The English Provinces c. 1760–1960. A Study in Influence (New York, 1964).
Robbins, Caroline, *The Eighteenth Century Commonwealthman* (Cambridge, Mass., 1959).
Roberts, David, *Victorian Origins of The British Welfare State* (New Haven, 1960).
Roberts, Michael, *The Whig Party, 1807–1812* (London, 1965).
Romilly, Samuel, *Memoirs* (3 vols.) (London, 1840).
Semmel, Bernard, *Imperialism and Social Reform, English Social–Imperial Thought, 1895–1914* (New York, 1968).
Thayer, George, *The British Political Fringe* (London, 1965).
Thomis, Malcolm I., *The Luddites* (Newton Abbot, 1970).
Thompson, E. P., *The Making of The English Working Class* (London, 1963).
Thompson, Laurence, *Robert Blatchford: Portrait of an Englishman* (London, 1951).

Thornton, A. P., *The Habit of Authority, Paternalism in British History* (London, 1965).
Veitch, G. S., *The Genesis of Parliamentary Reform* (Hamden, Conn., 1965).
Wallas, Graham, *The Life of Francis Place* (4th ed.) (London, 1925).
Walmsley, Robert, *Peterloo: The Case Reopened* (Manchester, 1969).
Watson, J. S., *The Age of George III* (Oxford, 1960).
West, J., *A History of The Chartist Movement* (New York and Boston, 1920).
White, R. J., *Waterloo to Peterloo* (London, 1957).

ARTICLES

Church, R. and Chapman, S. D., 'Gravener Henson and The Making of The English Working Class', Jones, E. L. and Mingay, G. E. (eds.), *Land, Labour and Population in The Industrial Revolution* (New York, 1967).
Foord, Archibald S., 'The Waning of the Influence of the Crown', *The English Historical Review*, vol. LXII (1947).

SERIAL PUBLICATIONS

Beginning in 1806 Cobbett's *Political Register* contains many references to Cartwright. Wooler's *Black Dwarf* was the Major's chief newspaper supporter from 1817 to 1824. However, the publishers of most radical papers had their own axes to grind and Cartwright remained his own best publicist.

INDEX

For EU product safety concerns, contact us at Calle de José Abascal, 56–1°, 28003 Madrid, Spain or eugpsr@cambridge.org.

www.ingramcontent.com/pod-product-compliance
Ingram Content Group UK Ltd.
Pitfield, Milton Keynes, MK11 3LW, UK
UKHW012339130625
459647UK00009B/393